COLOUR

YOUR HOME

COLOUR

YOUR HOME

Inspiring ideas to brighten up your life

Sally Walton

p

This is a Parragon Book

First published in 2002

Parragon

Queen Street House

4 Queen Street

Bath BA1 1HE, UK

Created and produced for Parragon by The Bridgewater Book Company Ltd.

Hardback ISBN: 0-75258-658-0

Paperback ISBN: 0-75258-659-9

Printed in China

Contents

Introduction

 Colour is something we take very much for granted because everything we see has a colour as well as a shape and size. Some people say they dream in black and white, but in fact our only concept of a world without colour comes from seeing old films or black and white photographs. This book will help you to look beyond the paint charts and fabric swatches for inspiration and, in doing so, discover how to use colour to make your home a happier, more comfortable and more stylish place to live.

ABOVE **Use of a bold primary colour on nearly every surface may not appeal to everyone as a decorating option. If the colour is applied with confidence, however, the results can be stunning, and certainly make a strong statement, often reflecting the personality of a room's occupant. The vibrant red used here brings life to an otherwise austere kitchen, and light flooding in through the large window makes the room glowing and cosy.**

COLOUR CHOICES

Colour surrounds us everywhere we look. From an early age we are asked to make colour choices, starting with a favourite crayon or pot of paint. We soon have such strong preferences that we throw tantrums unless we can wear our favourite yellow T-shirt or green jumper, whatever the weather. Decorating choices generally come later, although many kids watch decorating programmes and have strong opinions about which colours they want on their bedroom walls. Bold colour choices come naturally to kids and they usually take the 'money is no object' approach to the budget as well.

This book aims to help you make the colour decisions that suit you and your lifestyle best. If, for example, you work hard and need a relaxing environment to come home to, then aquamarines, lilacs or shades of blue will provide a calm atmosphere.

The first chapter explains the basics of colour theory and how all colours are derived from the three primary colours red, yellow and blue, from which are then created the secondary colours of orange, green and violet. In the second chapter we explore the relationship between colour and our emotions. Colour has many cultural and religious associations, and we also have instinctive preferences – positive associations and memories persuade us to choose one colour over another. Understanding our influences will help us to make the colour choices that suit our personalities.

Seeking a little natural inspiration for colour schemes is always a good idea – after all, nature is without inhibition, and rarely gets it wrong. A stroll in the country at different times of the year will provide endless possibilities.

BOTTOM Fruits and vegetables come in a whole range of marvellous colours, from the hot, vivid red and fresh, bright green of chillies to the soft orange of the inside of a mango or the sumptuous, rich purple of an aubergine. Spend some time in a vegetable market for some great decorating ideas.

In the third chapter we look at textures and special effects, and how they can be used to add depth to our decorating. The next chapter offers practical projects that will help to transform your home and presents ideas for adding focal points of colour to a room.

All colours exist naturally in an enormous range of variations, and a glance at a summer garden in full leaf will reveal that each species of plant is a different shade of green. When we describe colours to each other without the benefit of a photograph we use all kinds of references to conjure up a picture in the mind's eye. A certain shade of pink may be described as looking like the inside of a seashell or as the colour of unpainted plaster or of bougainvillaea flowering on a white wall. We store colour and texture memories; it is often the combination of the two that brings a colour to mind.

Inspiration for colour schemes can be drawn from many sources other than the conventional magazines or colour swatch cards. Look at the colours of fruit in the market or of tropical fish in an aquarium. You may be drawn to a painting or perhaps just one area of it because the colours look so good together.

Choosing a colour scheme that is the height of fashion has many advantages – the paint colours will be readily available, your home will look fresh and up-to-date and the shops will be full of colour coordinating accessories. Home colour fashions change less often than they do for clothes, but there is a strong connection. The colours you see on the catwalks one year may just turn up in the DIY store the next.

The book does not deal only with ideas and theories about colour; there are also plenty of practical, easy-to-follow projects, all of which are based around a colour theme. Each one has been designed to be quick and easily accomplished and to give maximum impact for minimum effort. There is a range of soft furnishing, painting, craft and styling projects, so there should be something to suit all tastes. I hope that you find it useful, stimulating and fun to read and that you turn to it often for inspiration.

Colour and Design

Choosing the right colour combinations for our homes will undoubtedly help us to create rooms that make us feel good. We all have personal favourites; for example, we choose our clothes from a mixture of our instinctive colour preferences and what is currently fashionable. Where decorating is concerned, however, the stakes are higher, because mistakes can be both expensive and time-consuming. It makes sense to use some of your planning time to find out more about colour and how it can be used to the most positive effect in your home. This first chapter introduces the basic principles of colour theory, explaining why some colours blend comfortably when seen alongside each other, while others appear to vibrate and create visual friction.

Understanding the colour wheel

Colour breathes life into a home. It can warm or cool, calm or excite us. Clever use of colour can make small rooms look more spacious or cavernous rooms feel cosy. It can blank out unsightly features and bring the ornate and interesting ones sharply into focus. It has the potential to elevate and energise all your interior decorating. Never before have home decorators had this much colour choice, and the ranges just keep growing – often leading to more confusion and indecision. How can we select colours that are right for us?

COLOUR THEORY

Knowing some basic colour theory will help you to make colour choices that go beyond your gut reaction to a colour scheme, although that is also hugely important. Basic colour tricks and rules exist, and it is certainly useful to take some time to understand them, even if in the end you decide to break all the rules. Colour has always been a tool for self-expression!

Three hundred years have passed since Sir Isaac Newton shone pure white light through a glass prism onto a neutral background and was delighted to see a continuous band of merging colour ranging from red through orange, yellow, green, blue and violet. In essence he had captured a miniature version of the rainbow, which is created by light passing through drops of rain, causing the spectrum colours to be projected like a giant colour slide across the sky.

THE COLOUR WHEEL

The colour wheel is the standard way to explain colour mixing by separating the spectrum into twelve different colours. At the centre of the wheel is a triangle divided into three equal sections of the primary paint colours – red, yellow and blue.

These three colours are called primary because they cannot be obtained from a mixture of any other colours. Along with black and white, they form the basis of all other paint colours.

RIGHT **Yellow, red and blue are the primary colours on which the colour wheel is based.**

When colours are arranged as a colour wheel, it helps us to understand their relationships to each other and the different effects that are produced when they are used alongside and opposite each other.

Secondary colours are produced by mixing two primary colours:
- yellow + red = orange
- yellow + blue = green
- blue + red = violet.

Tertiary colours are made by mixing a secondary colour with an equal amount of the colour next to it on the wheel:
- yellow + orange = yellow orange (golden yellow)
- red + orange = red orange (burnt orange)
- yellow + green = yellow green (lime green)
- blue + green = blue green (turquoise)
- blue + violet = blue violet (indigo)
- red + violet = red violet (crimson).

It is also useful to discover how much or how little of one colour is added to another to make a third colour. Try making your own colour wheel.

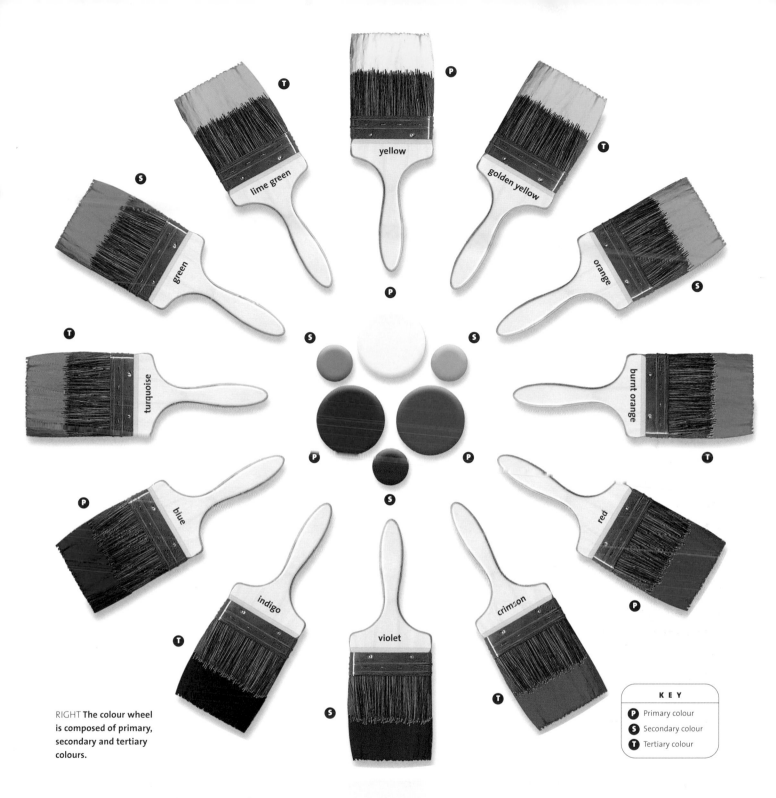

RIGHT **The colour wheel is composed of primary, secondary and tertiary colours.**

KEY
P Primary colour
S Secondary colour
T Tertiary colour

HOW TO MAKE A COLOUR WHEEL

1 Begin with a large dab each of primary red, yellow and blue paint in the middle of a white plate, with yellow at the top, red lower right and blue in the lower left. These are the **primary** colours and will form the basis of your colour wheel.

2 Now mix an equal amount of primary colour into the one next to it, around the outside of the original three colours. You will produce orange, green and violet. These **secondary** colours fill the spaces midway between each two primaries.

3 Place a dot of each primary colour on the plate rim opposite its central position, and do the same with the secondary colours. Leave a space between each large enough for the **tertiary** colours (made by mixing a secondary colour with an equal amount of the colour next to it on the wheel).

Colour – our visual experience

Colour is a very powerful tool that can be used effectively to help signs or signals convey their message. Our experience of colour varies depending on the amount of light available, so the use of colour varies accordingly. During daylight hours, for example, we experience the contrast of yellow and black very strongly, and these colours may be used for warning signs. At night we can see red without making any adjustment to our eyes, so it is ideal for warning lights on cars and to signal 'stop' at traffic lights.

ABOVE **It is possible to drive a car safely at speed along a busy highway at night because of coloured rear lights. The red lights are easily read by our eyes in darkness, making it possible immediately to recognise and react to brake and indicator lights.**

SIGNS AND SIGNALS

Our eyes experience colours as wavelengths of light, with each colour having its own frequency that is recognised and interpreted by the brain. The paint colours used for public information signs, logos, advertising and packaging are not chosen at random. They have been deliberately selected, using scientifically proven data, to be the most effective colour for the purpose and situation.

In daylight, for example, yellow is most instantly readable and yellow and black give the strongest contrast, so these colours are used on construction vehicles, barriers and warning signs.

Green on white, red on white, white on blue and black on white also have immediate impact. Poor combinations in daylight are red on blue, red on green and blue on green.

On its own, red-orange grabs our attention, and this makes it ideal for sea rescue craft. Red also advances, and is transmitted on the highest frequency of all colours; it is immediately recognised, making it the obvious choice for the stop signal at the traffic light.

We see coloured light in different ways, and in daylight yellow/green is brightest; in low light blue/green is most visible; but in extreme darkness our eyes see red light clearly without having to make any adjustment, and this is why red light is used for controls and warnings that need to be clear at night.

LEFT Here mother nature's warning colours yellow and black are used to reinforce the skull and crossbones danger message.

RIGHT A red circle with a line passing through it is universally understood as a prohibition message. Red signals danger and the precise nature of the message is described by the black Icon.

A TRICK OF THE LIGHT

The existence of colour depends entirely upon light. Try placing a red vase on a table in a room directly lit by a standard tungsten bulb. Turn the light off and the vase looks just as black as everything else in the dark room. The colour of any object is a visual experience and not a fact! We see this every day when the sun sets and darkness falls outside the window, yet the simple statement that colour is just a trick of the light is almost impossible to accept.

It is all to do with the power of a surface to absorb or reflect light particles.

Red appears to be red because it absorbs all the other colours of the spectrum and reflects only the red. Shine a green light onto a red object and it will no longer be red but black.

Anyone who has made the mistake of buying all red lights for their Christmas tree will confirm the strangely deadening effect they have on the green of the tree, and the way they rob the ornaments of their sparkle.

Colour is a powerful tool that works on many different levels – and the more you know about colour, the more chance you have of using it to its full potential.

A red light shining on this vase and flower intensifies the red and knocks out the green.

The green light enriches all the green and tints the background.

In a blue light the red flowers lose their red glow; the vase becomes more turquoise.

Yellow light warms the red to orange and turns the vase a sickly green. It is never flattering.

Halogen lights are bright and give off a bright white light that does not affect colour.

Tungsten lights are no-frills everyday light bulbs. They give out a pleasant glow.

Colour terms

The language used to describe colour includes some specific terms that you may not have come across before unless you have studied art or interior design. The few terms that are explained here are those that are most likely to be mentioned within the context of home decorating. Some specialist terminology will come in handy and make it much easier to communicate your thoughts and ideas about colour when dealing with professionals in the industry.

LEFT **Golden yellow and mauve clash with each other, producing a kind of visual discomfort.**

BELOW **Blue and orange appear directly opposite each other on the colour wheel and are known as complementary colours.**

ADDITIVE COLOUR

This is the colour of light, where adding all the colours together creates white light.

CLASHES OR DISCORDS

This describes two colours of equal intensity, which cause visual discomfort. Think of them as musical harmonies and discords. Designers and artists sometimes make use of this effect to create a disturbance and give the colour scheme an 'edge', and colour clashes were most famously used in the rebellious 1960s – bright orange and shocking pink, for instance, or golden yellow and mauve.

COMPLEMENTARY COLOURS

Colours opposite each other on the colour wheel are called 'complementary'. These are colours of equal intensity. When they are combined in equal proportions they make a neutral grey. When placed alongside each other, they achieve maximum intensity and compete for attention.

ABOVE In the black and white half of this picture the light foreground and dark background are very clearly defined. In the coloured half the tonal contrasts are not as obvious because the glow from the bright yellow illuminates the wall.

CONTRASTS

Hue

The simplest contrast to understand is that of hue, which describes the difference between undiluted colours seen alongside each other. The primary colours (yellow, red and blue) are the most extreme example.

Hot and cold

Some colours are hot – red, yellow and orange; some are cold – blue, green and violet. The most extreme hot/cold contrasts are red-orange and blue-green.

Light and dark

Light and dark contrast is clear when you look at a colour and a black-and-white version of the same photograph. Red and green have the same tonal quality and show up as an equal grey. Yellow and violet are the most extreme examples of this contrast (apart from black and white, which are not colours, but tones).

HUE

A hue is one of the pure colours of the spectrum, like red or yellow, and it can be used to describe the character of another colour – for example, lavender has a violet hue, olive has a green hue or pink has a red hue.

HARMONIES

A harmony is a combination of colours that allows the eye to travel smoothly between them with no sharp contrasts. Colours that are close to each other on the colour wheel will naturally harmonise – yellow, orange and red, for example.

INTENSITY

This describes how much pigment is in the paint. The more pigment there is, the stronger and less diluted the colour will be. Another word used to describe colour intensity is saturation.

NEUTRALS

These are black, white, grey, beige and cream.

SURFACE COLOUR OR PAINT COLOUR

This is colour that is mixed from pigments, where adding all the primary colours together creates black. This is the colour we deal with when decorating, which differs from the colours of light. When all the primary colours of light are combined, the resulting light is white.

TINTS AND SHADES

The addition of white to a colour produces a tint, which we call a pastel colour; and black darkens a colour to produce a shade.

ABOVE These three blocks are an example of subtle tints and shades. The central colour has been lightened by tinting with white (left) and darkened by adding a small amount of black (right).

Classic colours

 The colours people choose to decorate their homes are usually muted, light and easy on the eye. This type of decorating does not follow fashion and has been around for decades. Classic combinations like pale blue and white with yellow highlights or terracotta and blue grey with cream almost carry a guarantee of success. These schemes work because the colours look good together, balance each other and are easy to live with. These schemes are not dull, because colours can be arranged in many ways.

TRIED AND TESTED COLOUR SCHEMES

These colour schemes combine harmonious colours with similar tonal values, usually with pale neutral or white for the woodwork. Any deeper colours are introduced by way of soft furnishings and accessories. The effect is pleasing and easy to live with.

Complementary colour schemes built around contrasting hues only work well when one colour is dominant and the other is used to complement it – for example, red lampshades and cushions in a predominantly green room.

Magnolia – pale beige with a hint of pink – is famously inoffensive. But it was too successful; new designers railed against safe colours, and magnolia became synonymous with being boring.

Monochromatic or **single-colour** schemes rely on using one hue in different tones and intensity. This creates a strong sense of style, but also requires a disciplined lifestyle, as colourful clutter tends to detract from the look.

ABOVE The walls have been colour-washed with a pale blue over cream and the main furnishings keep to the blue theme. The floor is of honey-toned parquet tiles and the natural wooden furniture has been kept light, giving a harmonious effect.

RIGHT The deep emerald green walls give this otherwise traditional living room a warm and intimate atmosphere. The curtain and cushion fabric picks up the green and the bright red adds a complementary balance. Pools of light from the lamps and the fire's glow make this room cosy.

COLOUR AND CLIMATE

Climate has a big effect on colour choices. Countries nearest the equator use the most brilliant colours because of the bright sunlight – pale colours and subtle tones and shades would not be visible under such intense light. In the north, where the sunlight is less powerful, bright colours seem harsh and brash, but pale, more subtle colours look their best. This is why attempts to recreate a paradise island on a chilly hillside in the north of Scotland are doomed to failure.

In Scandinavia, where the winters are long and cold, the popular decorating style is surprisingly minimalist. In traditional homes, walls are painted pale blue or white, with pale natural wooden floors. The modern Swedish style retains the clean open look, but uses brighter colours, especially yellow.

In North Africa, house exteriors tend to be painted with earth colours, but the interiors are a riot of jewel-bright colours. Decoration features elaborate geometric tiling and panelling. Deep intense blue, viridian green, golden yellow and rose pink are painted onto walls and used in geometric patterns.

In the Greek Islands, houses are painted white to deflect the heat of the sun. Windows are small, which makes interiors quite dark and gloomy, but cool. The traditional colour for woodwork is bright blue, which the sun fades to a wonderful aquamarine. The sight of bright pink geraniums blooming on balconies and doorsteps alongside this blue and white is simply beautiful.

India, of all places in the world, is most associated with brilliant colours. The colour combinations on the exteriors of houses can be literally dazzling. Peppermint green and vivid mauve and shocking pink seem to look perfect next to emerald green, carmine red and saffron yellow. The rules are that there are no rules – and it looks divine.

Colours that go together

 The question most people ask when wading through colour charts is: 'Do you think these two colours will go together?' A good approach to the answer is to leave the technicalities aside and look at some tried and tested colour schemes. Look somewhere other than a paint chart. If you see a grey slate rooftop against a pale blue sky or a purple wisteria plant tumbling over a soft yellow stone wall, make a mental note of the colours that appeal to you and consult the paint charts with this image in mind.

Contemporary

Yellow and blue are a positive, uplifting and friendly combination of colours. The walls here are a bright sunflower yellow, which glows under the spotlights and is complemented by the deep blue of the table top. The yellow looks equally good with the enamelled surface of the light-blue cooking range, the natural wood and the reflective chrome. The kitchen is busy and filled with interestingly shaped objects wrapped up into one harmonious package by the glowing yellow backdrop.

COLOUR KEY

1. Ink blue
2. Light blue
3. Sunshine yellow

Traditional

This elegant room has been decorated in a classic pale blue, white and gold scheme. The fireplace, ceiling and built-in cupboards are all matt white set against duck egg blue walls. The room has a good floor that has been stripped and polished and, along with the faded antique rug, it provides the room with warmth. The combination of black and gold candlesticks, gilt frames, wire mesh cupboard doors and the gilded chair give the room a classic French style, which provides an understated background for well chosen elements.

COLOUR KEY

1. Ice blue
2. Matt white
3. Yellow ochre

Natural

Where flowers grow in their natural habitat, the colours are in harmony with their surroundings. The colours of the landscape and plant life are a source of constant inspiration. Think of heather on the moors set against a pale sky, daisies in the grass, bluebells carpeting the woods or primroses on mossy banks, or the place where the sea meets the shore.

You just can't go wrong if you choose your colour scheme this way.

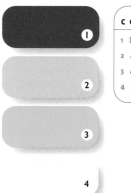

COLOUR KEY

1 Deep blue
2 Aqua
3 Apple
4 Pale apple

COLOUR COMBINATIONS IN NATURE

Two light neutrals and one strong colour

❋ White + grey + yellow

❋ Cream + stone + Sienna red

❋ Sand + cream + sky blue

Similar subdued tones of contrasting colours with a light neutral

❋ Sage green + brick red + light stone

❋ Wedgwood blue + apricot + creamy white

Similar tones of harmonious colours with a deep tone of one

❋ Pale blue + lavender + deep purple

❋ Apricot + shell pink + deep ruby red

❋ Sage green + yellow-cream + deep green

Different tones of a single colour with a light neutral

❋ Mid blue + pale blue + cream with gold highlights

❋ Mint green + emerald green + white

❋ Deep + pale orange + soft grey

Earth tones

❋ Yellow ochre + brown + red ochre + pale honey

❋ Stone + grey + black + yellow ochre + red ochre

Naturals

❋ Light + deep olive green + mud-brown + off-white

❋ Cream + dark brown + pale straw + silver green

Personal taste

If you were to start with a clean slate and were able to reinvent your personal taste, the result is likely to be as sterile as a hotel room or a room set in a furniture showroom. These rooms, designed to make many different people feel at home, always lack the character of personal expression. Taste evolves with us, whether as a result of rejecting our parents' taste or being strongly influenced by fashion or a particular era's decorating style. Our taste in colours also builds up over the years and is developed from an accumulation of influences that go back to childhood.

A BACKGROUND TO YOUR LIFE

Visualise a living room with a white ceiling, pale blue walls, white woodwork and natural polished wood flooring. This is a traditional classic colour scheme, chosen to provide an unobtrusive background for elegant furniture – perhaps some antiques and paintings, and a chandelier. Now place your own furniture in the room and imagine how it will look.

Picture the same room with the skirting and window frames painted a deep turquoise blue and the walls sunshine yellow. Is this more your sort of look? This is an extreme version of a very useful exercise, because the things you already own and love can provide the best clues when you are looking for a new colour scheme.

The front door makes the first statement about who lives behind it, and your colour choice can advertise or conceal your personality. Vivid orange, bright golden yellow or scarlet announce flamboyance and sociability; and deep green suggests a much calmer welcome.

Busy rooms – like family kitchens, where there is a constant flow of traffic and activity – benefit from bold colours and strong contrasts, which add to the room's dynamism. Hallways look inviting in warm yellow or burnt orange, whereas a bedroom is more relaxing if painted a calming green, meditative blue or lilac.

The way your house functions is improved by the colours chosen for rooms and connecting areas.

LEFT **The detail of this fine old chair would be lost if set against a bright patterned wallpaper. Design your colour schemes to flatter the furniture or objects you already own.**

RIGHT **This rough distressed wall finish is a perfect background for a contemporary folding chair. The different textures create a contradiction that gives the image energy. The very old and very new often make good companions.**

Art Deco

In the 1920s the Art Deco style was one of symmetry, stepped shapes, vertical lines and smooth surfaces. The style was influenced by the Cubist art movement and the arrival of the movies and the great ocean liners. Chrome, glass, ceramics, marble and leather were some of the most popular ingredients. This was an era when 'having style' was considered a top priority This room features a classic 1920s fireplace and a stunning circular ceiling.

COLOUR KEY

1 Cream
2 Plaster pink
3 Warm orange

Diner-style

The 1950s style is bold and fun. In the 1950s, decorating celebrated the return of colour after the drab war years, and many of the innovations that had focused on the military were at the disposal of designers for the home market. The plastics industry celebrated with coloured laminated surfaces and moulded plastic shapes. Chrome kitchen appliances echoed the shapes of streamlined cars and planes and black and white checked patterns added style.

COLOUR KEY

1 Ketchup red
2 Gloss white
3 Black

FAVOURITISM

We all favour certain colours, and consequently no amount of theoretical knowledge is going to convince someone to paint a room purple if they are of a pastel pink persuasion.

Vive la différence! Each of us is unique, and personal taste varies enormously.

FOLLOWING FASHION

Decorating has always followed fashion. Fashions used to be dictated by kings and queens and ignored at your peril. Scarcity of certain pigments played a large part in how and where they were used, until the Victorians invented synthetic colour dyes. Initially pigments were made from earth, minerals or plants; some were rare and expensive. Blue and purple are two colours whose rarity ensured that they were reserved for royalty and deity, and they still hold these associations today.

These days we are more likely to be influenced by top fashion designers, whose work often encompasses interiors and home accessories. This cross-over has introduced an aspirational feeling to interior decorating and spawned many magazines. Fashion is fun and, because it is ever-changing, it is also refreshing. The latest colour scheme can certainly bring a drab room right up to date, but it is important to avoid being a fashion victim. Decorating is big business – to keep the tills ringing, paint companies also ring the colour changes every season. But stick to what you like and what suits your room – unless you feel like a change!

Pattern and texture

 A colourful room without textural contrasts would look strangely sterile. The texture of an object is one of our key descriptive tools, and a surface pattern can be used to enhance a shape or carry a colour scheme. When solid colour seems heavy and overpowering over large areas, a patterned version can give a much lighter feel. The dense texture of a carpet means a plain colour often works well on the floor but patterns might work better for curtains or wallpaper.

Faux linen: denim blue is a good colour for upholstery.

Faux snakeskin: chenille printed in a python pattern.

Woven chenille: a flat weave fabric with a very soft texture.

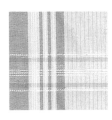

Woven check: in harmonious orange, yellow and cream.

Cotton/linen: embodying the English country-house style.

Kasbah: this pattern motif works well with a traditional style.

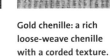

Jacquard weave: a hard-wearing fabric good for upholstery.

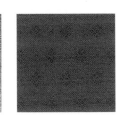

Leather: the most hard-wearing of all upholstery material.

Gold chenille: a rich loose-weave chenille with a corded texture.

Woven dobby: fabric that has the look of brushed denim.

Suede fabric: the look of real suede and a smooth texture.

PATTERN

Interior decorating styles follow catwalk fashions, and most of the top clothes designers now also have home ranges that include furniture, carpets, fabrics and paint colours. So it is possible to co-ordinate every area of your life in the style of someone with impeccable design credentials! In real life, few of us would go that far – but it is useful to keep an eye on fashion, where you will find clues to new colour trends. Pattern has been kept to a minimum for a long time, but that is about to change, and this is good for home decorators. Pattern is a great way of introducing more colour into a room.

TEXTURE

The texture of a colour can change its appearance more than you would imagine. Some colours look bland and dead when painted in a matt emulsion. Terracotta is a good example of this, as it only comes to life on a rough rustic surface or when used as a patchy colourwash. Mint green is another example – it looks fresh and fantastic in a chalky finish, but safe and dull in a flat emulsion. Some colours benefit from having a reflective sheen, especially in combination with a contrasting matt colour. Matt chocolate-brown woodwork with a glossy cream wall looks really delicious, and red always looks better with a sheen. The deep green of glass bottles is stunning with light shining through it, but the colour is nothing without transparency and light. Experiment with sample pots if you are unsure about which texture of paint will give the look you're after.

A room style based on a natural palette where there is little colour variation is brought to life by different textures, such as woven wool, linens and cottons, sisal matting, sheepskin, leather, bleached wood and glass. A very little colour will go a long way when a rich variety of textures provides the visual interest.

ABOVE **In this room the chalky texture of the walls has been emphasised by the use of a high sheen paint for the dado rail. Chalk finish paints dry to a paler version of the applied colour and have a soft, powdery surface bloom. Any type of paint can be given a glossy finish by applying a coat of clear gloss varnish.**

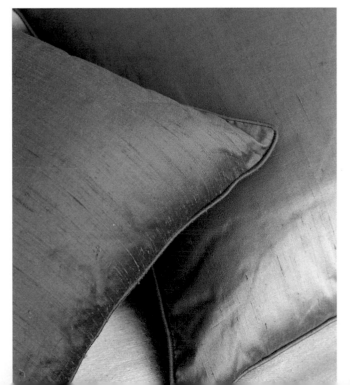

LEFT **Cushions are the easiest way to introduce different textures and colours to a room. Look for cushion fabrics with an obviously contrasting texture to the furniture upholstery, such as these shiny Shantung silks against the unbleached rough linen of the sofa.**

Contemporary colour schemes

If you follow fashion and want the latest look, a fresh coat of paint is the cheapest, quickest and easiest way to change the look of a room. Think about the atmosphere you want in your room, and choose the colours accordingly. Most paint companies produce ranges of co-ordinating colours with different contemporary theme names – tropical, spicy, natural, ethnic and so on. If you are after a contemporary style, then look no further; these ranges represent the most popular looks of the moment.

PAINT EFFECTS

Paint effects no longer require specialist materials – most companies have a range of products that enable beginners to apply colour in effects such as metallic, denim, linen, suede, rustic or antique. No more excuses – it's time to strip the varnish off the pine kitchen units and update them with coloured woodwash.

COLOUR KEY

1 Aluminium
2 Deep lavender
3 Pale lilac

Metallics

Zinc, chrome, stainless steel and copper have all crossed over from the factory into the home, providing a fresh, young style that does not cost a fortune. Metallic doesn't have to mean cold hard steel any more either, as there are several excellent metallic acrylic paint ranges on the market that can be used on most surfaces, including walls and furniture. Look no further than this if you have a boring chest of drawers in need of an update. Here the handles have been replaced with half-moon cut-outs, and the wood surface painted shimmering silver.

Jewel-bright colours

Jewel-bright colours make a big impact, and look fabulous with unfussy furniture and equally vibrant fabrics, like Indian sari silks or South American woven textiles. The way to use jewel colours is to choose mainly harmonising shades like crimsons, reds and oranges with small amounts of equally intense contrasts. Avoid using equal amounts of intense contrasting colour like orange and blue or red and green, as they can actually cause visual discomfort. Keep the colours flowing through the room by picking them up with accessories such as cushions, throws and lampshades.

COLOUR KEY

1 Rich red
2 Salmon pink
3 Deep golden yellow

Chalky colours

Chalky colours create a soft, matt texture. They are usually mixed with water before application, and you can vary their strength from a thick textured matt covering to a soft colourwash. The colours dry lighter, with a soft bloom on the wall's surface. Bright chalky colours give a youthful, Caribbean island look – imagine a bright but sun-bleached beach house veranda, bright blue sky and palm trees. Pale chalky colours are cool and sophisticated, perfect for the sort of people who don't need wipe-clean surfaces!

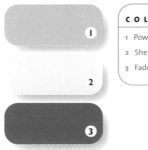

COLOUR KEY

1 Powder pink
2 Sherbert yellow
3 Faded denim

Creating an illusion

 Colour can be a magical tool if you have awkwardly proportioned rooms, as often happens when houses are converted into flats. When big rooms are divided up, high ceilings can make them look smaller than they are. This is where clever use of colour comes in useful.
If a room has unusual proportions, colour is the cheapest way to improve it without structural alterations. Light colours reflect the most light, making rooms appear bigger and brighter, while dark colours have the opposite effect.

TRICKS OF THE TRADE

A very high ceiling can be made to look a lot lower if a light colour is used on the walls up to the height where the ceiling would be in proportion with the room, then a dark colour is used above it for the top part of the walls and the ceiling. Fix a chandelier to hang into the room below the dark top section and the high ceiling will 'appear to disappear'. If you prefer not to have a central light, then make a feature of the lighting by using sculptural contemporary lights to create focal points where you choose to have them, or large table lamps that shed pools of light to give a cosy atmosphere. Look out for the new rechargeable coloured balls of light – the charge lasts about four hours, and nobody will ever notice your high ceiling!

A low ceiling will look higher if the walls are painted in a dark colour or papered with a 'busy' patterned paper up to dado rail height, then painted a very light colour above it, including the ceiling. Lighting and colour can help exaggerate the illusion of space. Harness blue's receding quality and use subtle washes of light from uplighters to add the most height, like looking up into a pale summer sky. For a fantastic contemporary design solution, try soft washes of slowly changing coloured light on a white ceiling to turn your low ceiling into an art feature. Specialist lighting shops have the necessary equipment, and they are a lot less rare than they used to be.

ABOVE **Faced with a room with fine proportions like this one, it would have been a pity to spoil the symmetry by boxing in pipework. The far more sympathetic and successful alternative was simply to paint the pipes to match the background. This works particularly well with a matt paint finish because the shapes don't catch the light.**

LEFT **One way to create a harmonious home is to link the colours of one room with the corridor, stairway or a feature in the next room. Here the staircase is painted to match the woodwork in the foreground and a band of the blue along the top of the skirting or string echoes the room's wall colour.**

OPTICAL ILLUSIONS

• If the room is long and narrow, it can be made to look wider by painting the longer walls with a cool pale green or blue, so that the walls appear to recede. The narrower walls will appear to advance if you paint them in a deep, warm shade of red or red-brown.

• Paint corridors to harmonise with the room colour and remove doors to create a more open-plan sense of space in a small flat.

• Make 'small' a virtue by painting walls and ceilings of tiny rooms in deep warm colours for a wrap-around cosiness.

• Blot out unwanted details like pipework or damaged plaster features by painting them the same colour as the surroundings.

• Add interest to a square plain room by creating optical illusions with blocks of colour. Drop-shadows, stripes or stencilled mouldings can all be used in contemporary or traditional ways.

ABOVE **You can make a low ceiling seem higher by painting the walls in a dark colour and the ceiling in a pale colour or white.**

RIGHT **Painting the ceiling in a darker colour than the walls of a room will appear to reduce the height of the room and provide a more intimate atmosphere.**

Colour and light

 The appearance of a colour depends on the quality of the light it is seen in. Most of us share the experience of being unable to tell navy blue from black inside a store but once outside the blueness is revealed by daylight. Every colour can be enhanced, softened or highlighted with lighting. The combination of a warm colour scheme and soft lighting can create a relaxing environment, and cool colours with sharp contrasts and bright directional light can give a dull space an energetic uplift.

GETTING THE LIGHTING RIGHT

The boldest or most subtle colour scheme in the world looks the same in the dark – so it follows that getting the lighting right is absolutely vital. This means making the most of the natural light as well as using the best sort of artificial light for the effect you are after. Anyone who has visited a night club during the day will understand the magic of clever lighting, as daylight reveals what the lighting conceals. If your living room is the children's playroom during the day, then clever lighting tricks can help to create a more sensual atmosphere in the evening. Dimmer switches, uplighters and concealed lights will create soft ambient lighting conditions, and table lamps make pools of light that add intimacy to a room. Task spotlights can be used for 'work' areas such as hi-fi, TV and games consoles. Use small spots to accent flowers, art or any other features.

ABOVE, LEFT **Sunlight streams in through the gap between the muslin curtain and the window frame. The muslin softens the light that would otherwise dazzle in a white room. The floor is painted concrete and the walls whitewashed plaster yet the room has atmosphere created by the combination of a cotton rug, an attractive chair and the quality of the light.**

LEFT **Concealed neon tubes below the wall units illuminate this cool modern kitchen. Kitchens are often too bright but here the task lighting is concentrated on the work surfaces. The light bounces off the one emerald green wall, casting a cool, watery, green light on the whole room.**

LEFT Rich red walls and a dark rug surround this dining table. The spotlights are all focused on the tabletop, throwing the rest of the room into shadow and creating a sense of intimacy for an adult meal. The high chair in the background gives a hint that this room adopts a very different character during the day.

BELOW Yellow is the lightest and the brightest of the primary colours. It glows with reflected natural light and infuses the room with sunshine and warmth. The use of pink in the room beyond has an enticing effect when framed by the yellow.

A cool, north-facing room can be infused with warmth and light if you paint the walls warm light yellow, and any room will look lighter if you paint walls opposite the windows white or any other very light colour. If the windows are small, the natural light in the room will appear to double if the frame, recess and immediate surround are painted white.

Coloured glass or sheets of adhesive colour film applied to windows can change the room colour during the day. A white room can glow with pink, yellow or green when the sun shines through the glass, only to return to white again when the sun passes. In the same way, coloured lights can be used at night to change the mood and colour of a room. One London hotel has a range of coloured lighting options in every room, so guests can choose the room's colour mood.

Planning colour schemes

The starting point here is inspiration, and this could come from a room style seen in a magazine, a classic period style such as Regency, or the regional colours seen on a holiday abroad. Or it could be a combination of colours on a piece of fabric, in the corner of a painting, in a bunch of flowers, or in a bowl of fruit or sugared almonds – anything at all that pleases your eye and could be translated into colours for a room. Analyse the source of your inspiration to discover which of the colours will create the right mood.

SELECTION FACTORS

If the walls are to be all one colour, then it should work in context with all the above considerations. Lighter and darker versions of the same colour may be a better option, allowing some areas to appear more prominent than others.

Patterned wallpaper could also be used to add texture and variety without introducing another main colour. Bold patterns are back in fashion, and the right ones will certainly bring a room right up to date.

If you decide to base your colour scheme on an historical or regional style, the colour choices will be restricted to particular palettes. The colours simply have to be combined in the traditional way, and success is assured. Everything does not have to be innovative and original, and with colour schemes it is generally better to look at something that works well, then copy it.

Decide upon the main colours for the room. The walls, the ceiling, the floor and the woodwork are the key areas. Unless you are looking to create the illusion of a lower ceiling, then this should be the lightest colour in the room. The wall colour or colours can be either matt or have a slight sheen. The reflective sheen is best for pale colours where you want to increase the light in a room. Matt gives the most sophisticated look. Gloss is an unusual choice for walls but it is practical for hallways and stairways, especially when there are children in the house.

ABOVE **This rustic Mediterranean home is furnished with an eclectic mixture of art and country furniture. The room is whitewashed and the beams have been picked out in the brilliant blue typical of the region. Blue and white predominate for walls and woodwork, but the bright furnishings, pictures and flowers create a much more multicoloured look.**

ABOVE **Inspiration for planning your colour scheme can come from a wide variety of sources in your environment; make a collection of inspiring objects.**

features exist does not mean that they have to be picked out and contrasted with the wall colour.

Sometimes in a small room a more spacious, expansive effect is achieved by simply painting them the same colour as the walls, using an eggshell or satinwood paint. A large room, however, may benefit from the unifying effect of strong bands of colour at skirting, dado and picture rail height.

FLOORING

A new wooden floor will give any room a very clean, contemporary look, and the cost need not be exorbitant if you choose one of the cheaper laminates. It will provide a good base for colourful rugs, and the 'click' type of floorboards do not require glue and can be easily lifted and relaid elsewhere. If existing wooden floorboards are in reasonable condition, they can be painted or stripped and stained. This style of flooring is popular at the moment, and it can always be carpeted over in the future, so there is nothing to lose.

If new flooring is not an option, then the colour scheme will have to be chosen to take the existing flooring into account. If you have a rust-coloured carpet, for instance, choosing a contrast colour like light turquoise or ice blue for the walls will give you a much fresher, livelier effect than a more conventional harmonious yellow, cream or orange.

WINDOW FRAMES

Window frames are conventionally painted in a lighter colour than walls, as this reflects more light into the room. Unless they are an attractive key feature in the room, such as lovely old sashes or huge plate glass windows, the frames look better when kept light and neutral, as colour will make a feature of any defects.

SKIRTING BOARDS AND DADO RAILS

Skirting boards and dado or picture rails in older houses provide an opportunity for horizontal bands of colour to divide the walls in clean lines. Just because these

PATTERNS

If you would like to use a pattern, there are a few basic rules worth considering. Large patterns work best in large areas and small patterns are best suited to small areas where they can be appreciated. A small floral pattern will read as a texture from a distance, whereas a large floral repeat in a small area is far too overwhelming.

Geometric patterns have recently made a big comeback and, as an alternative to hanging wallpaper, a wall can be treated as a giant painter's canvas with stripes, circles and squares of colour.

Making a swatch board

Not only is this a useful exercise, but it is also great fun. It will help you to make the right choices if you are dealing with something tangible. Begin with your source of inspiration, whether this is a scrap of fabric, a postcard or a photograph you took on holiday. Place this onto a white background to isolate the colours. Take it with you to the paint store, and collect sample paint swatches that match, harmonise or contrast with it. Look at several different manufacturers' ranges as the colours vary a lot.

ABOVE **This is a swatch board created for a long sunny sitting room with a dining area at one end. The two main colours were used to homogenise the space, and differences in texture defined the areas. A detailed swatch board like this makes it easier to visualise the finished room.**

PAINTED SWATCHES

If your budget stretches to it, then also look at specialist ranges where the colours and finishes are often more unusual. Look out for painted swatches, which are far more accurate than the printed versions. If you are sensitive to chemicals, or simply wish to follow an environmentally kinder route, then send away for the 'greener' paint companies' colour cards.

Once you have found your colours, buy sample pots and paint them onto a piece of white board (at least 300mm sq./12in sq.) so you can see what the colour looks like, and whether it is true to the colour card. Placing the board opposite the window, and in a dark corner, will help you judge whether you could go lighter or darker without changing the colour. See what it looks like with things you will not change in the room.

Take the colour swatch with you when choosing fabric, wallpaper and carpets. Get samples of anything you like and put them together on the swatchboard. Once you have carpet, fabric and wallpaper, you will be able to see how the textures affect the colours. Refer back to your original inspiration and compare the colours to the ones that inspired you in the first place. If you haven't managed to find the right colours and you have time for more research, keep looking. There are more paint companies out there than you think, and it is usually the smaller, more specialist shops that deal in the desirable, unusual colours.

BRINGING IT ALL TOGETHER

When you have established your basic colour scheme
(walls, ceiling, flooring, woodwork, soft furnishings),
you can experiment with other textures, patterns and
colours for the accessories. It may be that a very muted
colour scheme needs a vibrant accent of colour to set it
off, or conversely that a gaudy background cries out for
a plain neutral rug or sofa. A newly painted bare room
can look unbearably bright until all your possessions are
back in place. Walls can be broken up with pictures,
lighting and shelves, and key wall colours can be picked
up on small items like vases, picture frames, cushions
and lampshades to create a more unified colour scheme.

ABOVE **A beautiful room, which demonstrates
successful use of colour in interior design. The walls
are painted a warm yellow-green, and the same
shade appears in the landscape painting. The
pictures are thoughtfully hung along a level base
line. The natural yellow pine floor is polished to a
high sheen to reflect and enhance the natural light,
and the rug frames the sleeping area. The simple
off-white grid pattern of the rug diffuses the
intense indigo blue, creating another level of low-
key pattern and colour interest. The bed linen in a
contrast of muted grey/white stripe and hot
salmon pink creates a seductive focal point. The
spiky bullrushes and the contemporary black lamp
perfectly balance each other's shapes. The room is a
wonderful example of harmony, balance and style.**

The Influences of Colour

Colour has a strong role to play in our lives, and can affect us both physically and psychologically. This chapter explores the ways different colours make us feel, and how a deeper understanding can help us to make positive use of this powerful tool. In the short term it can lift our spirits or help us to feel instantly relaxed, and in the long term it can be life-enhancing and even healing.

We may change the colours of our surroundings as an outward display of our personalities and preferences – this chapter offers a deeper understanding of colour selection.

Psychology of colour

Colour affects our states of mind; some even believe in its power to cure illness. Whether or not you believe in the more cosmic theories about colour, there is certainly scientific proof that colour can warm us up or cool us down. Using obvious literal associations, sunshine yellow makes us feel warm and deep blue cools us down. When the eye sees that lovely yellow, the brain interprets and associates it with warm sunshine, and the opposite happens with a cool icy blue – it's mind over matter.

FACTS AND FEELINGS

A scientific experiment involved a control group spending time at the same level of activity in the same workroom, painted first in cold colours and then in warm colours. The room temperature was gradually lowered; the level at which they first felt cold was 11°C/52°F in the red-orange room and 15°C/59°F in the blue-green room. It was concluded that colour has the power to increase or decrease the circulation, so it makes sense to paint a cold room in warm colours.

Scientists and psychologists have studied the subconscious aspects of colour's influence for many years, and most ancient civilizations used colour symbolically in art and decoration. Colours have both positive and negative associations – the positive side of yellow is warmth and sunshine, but it can also represent jealousy and cowardice. There are different cultural associations too – yellow is associated with spirituality in Buddhist countries, while in the Muslim world the holy colour is green. In France red symbolises masculinity, but in the rest of the world masculine is shown as blue.

Everyone understands that the expression 'feeling blue' means we are unhappy, just as 'seeing red' explains a feeling of rage. Other colours referred to in this way are 'green with envy', 'in the pink' (feeling flushed with good health) – and who can forget 'mellow yellow'?

Colour therapists believe in the healing power of coloured light. The treatment involves shining coloured lights on to the affected part of the body, with each colour having its own specialist area of healing activity. Colour is used for emotional, physical and spiritual healing, often in combination with crystals, astrology, acupuncture and traditional Eastern healing techniques.

LEFT **If you paint a cold room in a warm colour, such as red, you will create a room that is psychologically warm – it will be associated with flames, heat and fire.**

COLOUR ASSOCIATIONS

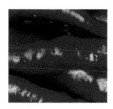

RED
- love • life • power • flames • heat
- rubies • roses • berries • blood
- danger • strength • hot chillies
- fire engines • sealing wax • Christmas
- revolution • sex • cherries

ORANGE
- oranges • tangerines • Chinese lanterns • pumpkins • clay • lentils
- spices • goldfish • marigolds • sunset
- terracotta • autumn leaves • amber
- marmalade • rust

BLACK AND WHITE
- the 1920s • the 1960s • tiled floors
- newsprint • photography
- chess boards • piano keys
- penguins

GREEN
- grass • leaves • ferns • cool • calm
- sea • hills • ecology • planet • growth
- tea • peppers • olives • avocados
- lizards • cactus • vegetables
- mint ice cream

AQUA AND TURQUOISE
- oceans • dreams • imagination
- sensitivity • freshness • holidays
- summer • mountain streams
- Navajo jewellery • Ancient Egypt

BLUE
- sea • sky • freshness • mountains
- cold • aquamarines • sapphires
- sadness • bluebells • ribbons • jeans
- berries • birds • heaven • duck eggs
- intelligence • calm

PURPLE
- robes • violets • plums • heather
- heliotrope • aubergine • passion
- sky • lilac • lavender • mourning
- luxury • grapes • psychics
- the Sixties

PALE PINK
- softness • baby girls • face powder
- meringues • sugared almonds
- strawberry ice cream • piglets • roses
- clouds • candy floss • fresh plaster
- sea shells

HOT PINK
- passion • heat • tropics • celebrations
- exotic flowers • lipstick • Indian saris
- Chinese lanterns • spices
- seaside rock • lobsters

METALLICS
- wealth • glamour • worship
- marriage • opulence • celebration
- luxury • solidity • weight • shimmer
- good luck

YELLOW
- sunshine • gold • straw • saffron
- bananas • custard • daffodils
- canaries • primroses • warmth
- ducklings • the moon

BROWN
- wood • coffee • chocolate • dogs
- horses • toffee • mushrooms • earth
- comfort • security • skin • velvet
- nuts • cookies

calming and relaxing

aqua and turquoise

Aqua and turquoise fall between blue and green, and carry with them all the positive aspects of those two colours. Aqua takes its name from the greenish blue of shallow water where the sea meets the sand, and shares it with a transparent gemstone of the same colour. Turquoise is the blue-green colour of an opaque semi-precious stone found in the Arizona desert. The Native American Navajo tribe believe that the colour has protective powers. So although the two colours are similar and often confused, one is fluid and transparent and the other opaque and solid.

The blue-greens are highly adaptable and look good both inside and outdoors, where their sparkle is not diminished by bright sunlight. Swimming pools are usually painted or mosaic-tiled in shades of turquoise blue because it makes the water look clean and inviting.

Aqua is the more dreamy of the two colours, and looks especially good with colours that have similar relaxing properties, such as the whole range of lavenders. This is a favourite colour for bathrooms, and cosmetic products are often packaged in shades of aqua for those wanting a co-ordinated look.

calming and relaxing: **aqua and turquoise**

COLOUR
PALETTE

Great combinations

Turquoise blue looks soft in pastel shades, and light turquoise has a contemporary edge when combined with rich earthy brown. Full-strength turquoise is best used on small areas where it packs a punch teamed with its complementary red-orange. Other earthy colours that look good with it are ochre yellow and Sienna red. Aqua works well for large areas, especially with a textured broken or chalky paint finish. In contrast, pale warm pink and terracotta suit it very well – and it looks great with icy sky-blue woodwork.

Naturally calm

The water in this mountain lake looks the purest transparent aquamarine. The clarity is a result of the fresh water being so clean and calm that it becomes a perfect reflector of the sky above. The pine trees around the edge of the lake are reflected in the water and add green to the blue, giving the water its amazing aquamarine colour.

COLOUR KEY

1 Prussian blue
2 Aqua
3 Apple
4 Pale lavender blue

Creating riches

These decorative papier-mâché containers have been painted with a combination of green and blue paint to create a rich turquoise effect. The colour can vary greatly, from a pale watery green to an intense bright blue. The effect is often lighter and purer if the colours are applied separately in glazes or washes rather than being pre-mixed. Metallic gold is the perfect complement to shimmering turquoise.

COLOUR KEY

1 Cobalt blue
2 Duck egg blue
3 Deep aqua
4 Hot pink

Tropical tones

The colour of the sea surrounding this tropical island is the most brilliant turquoise blue. The sand below is white and in the shallows the colour lightens to a pale aquamarine. These are the romantic colours of castaways, holidays and dreams.

COLOUR KEY

1 Aqua
2 Turquoise
3 Cobalt blue

calming and relaxing: **aqua and turquoise**

Setting the mood

Aqua as the main colour in a room gives it a cool, modern quality without any sense of there being a chill in the air. The touch of yellow in turquoise blue warms and mellows it, making it a very comfortable colour to live with. These colours are restful for our eyes and flattering to plain, uncluttered spaces. Keep to harmonising colours to preserve a restful atmosphere, or add a splash of complementary orange as a visual wake-up call. Aqua, yellow ochre and terra cotta create a warm Tuscan mood.

A touch of drama

This kitchen with aqua blue units and matching blinds set against a warm cream background is a good example of uncluttered, contemporary style. The strong ultramarine blue tiling adds depth with a flash of brilliance and the bright bowl of peppers provides a strong colour focal point. This is a good example of how dramatic but temporary colour such as fruit or flowers can be introduced to create a new dynamic in a room. The calming aqua is the main feature, with the jazzy colour of the peppers appearing in a cameo role.

COLOUR KEY
1 Shaker blue
2 Aqua green
3 Creamy white

Simply aqua

The all-over aqua blue, ceiling lights and spiky-leaved desert plants give this room the underwater atmosphere of an aquarium. The furniture style is ideally suited to the room. Imagine this setting in a house in the desert and you will appreciate the powerful influence that colour has on our senses. Stepping out of the heat and into this room would be instantly cooling and calming.

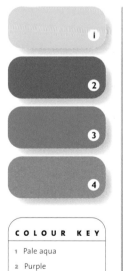

Clouds of colour

The intense aqua colour on the wall behind this lovely Art Nouveau style fireplace has been created by applying an emerald green glaze over a blue emulsion base coat, using a technique called 'clouding'. The glaze is spread with a soft cloth in a semi-circular motion to make subtle cloud-like shapes. The transparent colour glaze adds depth without obscuring the blue. The purple thistles and bright blue vase add lively sparks of colour to the black and white mantlepiece.

soothing and rejuvenating

pale pink

Pale pink is a wonderfully flattering colour. It seems to suit all complexions and bring a warm glow into any room. This is the colour of the inside of a seashell, apple blossom in springtime, strawberry ice cream and many other delicious and pretty things. Pink is always associated with sweetness and innocence. It is a life colour, a signal of health and well-being.

Pink is a colour well-suited for use over large areas. Its character is influenced by other colours – with dove grey, it is sophisticated; with pale lemon yellow, white and powder blue, it is nursery soft; but with faded aqua and terracotta red, it is typically Mediterranean. Pink is the natural colour of freshly plastered walls, a delicious warm earthy pink with a rustic character that is enhanced by deeper terracotta shades, natural wood and deep greens. Mixed with verdigris and ochre, it is reminiscent of faded pink villas on Tuscan hillsides.

Rosy pink is softer and sweeter, the colour of cascades of rambling roses around cottage doorways. Pink need not always be seen as exclusively feminine and can be very bold and striking in the deeper salmon shades that are tinged with orange.

soothing and rejuvenating: **pale pink**

Pleasing the senses

It is easiest to imagine a colour when we have several sensory references. We recall the taste, smell, appearance, sound and texture and create a perfect image in our mind's eye. It is impossible to think of sweet peas without also conjuring up their scent. Each of these pale pinks tickles the senses in a different way. Rose pink mixes well with deeper reds, white, sky blue, and pale and mid green. Salmon pink, black and cream create a smart look. Pale pink looks equally delicious in chalky distemper paint or high gloss.

Purely pink

The shape and texture of a meringue are unique. These sculptural mixtures of sugar and frothy egg whites set hard and crisp but dissolve at first bite into a chalky crumbling sweetness. The colour is a pale and pure mix of white sugar tinted with pink food colouring that always looks like the prize exhibit in the bakery window.

COLOUR KEY	
1	Plaster pink
2	Rosy pink
3	Salmon
4	Cool pale pink

Sweet inspiration

Sugared almonds in a bowl almost look as if they could have been laid by an exotic bird rather than made in a sweet factory. The set sugar coating has the smooth glazed appearance of marble and the pink seems to be tinted with a touch of cool blue. The paint equivalent of the surface is a satin finish that has a slight sheen but none of the vulgarity of a full gloss. This pink looks lovely alongside other pale pastels and white.

COLOUR KEY

1 Pale lemon

2 Pale lavender

3 Rosy pink

Baby soft

Only the softest of fabrics should be used to wrap up a tiny baby, and this pale pink blanket conjures up those delicate first months of life. It is a colour of life and of gentle energy.

COLOUR KEY

1 Pale soft pink

2 Rosy pink

3 Pale pink

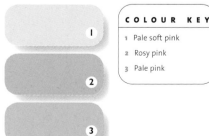

soothing and rejuvenating: **pale pink**

Soft or sophisticated

Pale pink is an undemanding colour to live with and is useful for softening hard edges and creating a rosy glow. It is an adaptable background colour that feels equally at home in the nursery or the office. Baby pink looks sweet with white or cream and other pastel shades, but it can also look sophisticated alongside steel grey; or funky with a sharp lime green or turquoise. Pale pink with black shouts 1950s glamour, pink gingham has a cute French style and plaster pink is popular in the Country Style palette.

COLOUR KEY	
1	Pale ochre yellow
2	Orange sorbet
3	Plaster pink
4	Hot pink

Deliciously pink

A delicious combination of pink and pale blonde wood that conjures up a vision of a strawberry ice cream with a fan-shaped wafer biscuit. The creamy pink is warmed by the soft light from above and by the reflected yellow tones of the wood. The chalky matt black pot adds a third but unobtrusive colour to this harmonious combination. The pale yellow twig arrangement is a perfect colour match for the wooden doors and their scratch patterned frame echoes the shape of the twigs.

Cool pink

Pale pink is given a contemporary treatment here by being teamed with grey woodwork and a simple pale pink curtain. The three pendant lights with brilliant blue glass shades create a cool modern look and the colour is picked up with the arrangement of blue glass on the window ledge.

COLOUR KEY

1　Plaster pink
2　Deep turquoise
3　Ultramarine

Pretty in pink

It would be difficult not to feel soothed and pampered in this pretty room. The walls are painted a very soft shell pink that reflects a soft pink glow onto the white bedstead. The bed linen is a mixture of harmonious pink and white stripes and florals.

COLOUR KEY

1　Shell pink
2　Pale creamy yellow
3　Rose pink

passionate
hot pink

Passionate pink is hot, feminine, spicy – and impossible to ignore. It is a courageous choice – a pink that will grant a room instant sex appeal and vitality. In nature it is the colour of brilliant desert cactus flowers, where maximum visibility is necessary to attract pollinating insects to ensure the plant's survival. Another hot location where it makes a big impression is as bougainvillaea trailing down whitewashed villa walls around the Mediterranean.

Pigments of the colour have been made in India and the Far East for centuries, giving it an exotic appeal to Westerners. The intensity of hot pink is seen at its best in Indian saris, Chinese silks and shimmering satins. It is also known as shocking pink. Needless to say, this is the perfect colour for a love nest, but it is also a fun colour to use in other parts of the home. Like red, hot pink will appear to shrink a room, so it should only be used where that is the desired effect.

In the East this colour is often used with gold, but this should be done sparingly, as a trimming, or the effect will be too brash. Keep the heat turned full on by mixing it with other strong colours like deep crimson red.

passionate: **hot pink**

COLOUR PALETTE

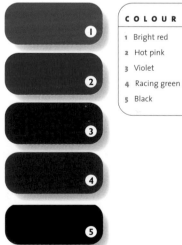

Causing a sensation

Walls painted with hot pink will advance to make a room look smaller. The pink will be 'grounded' and the room's original proportions restored if pale moss green is used on the woodwork – these colours work very well together. Hot pink with other jewel-bright colours like purple, emerald and peacock blue creates a vibrant ethnic look. Patterns of swirls, geometrics and stylised flowers in hot pink, yellow, orange, apple green and white proclaim an allegiance to 1970s' revival style.

Irresistibly pink

Bright passionate pink flowers are the first to catch the eye in the garden. The colour leaps forward to demand attention and needs to be used with some discriminaton if it is not to overwhelm a flowerbed. Hot pink anemone flowers with their large fringed black centres set against feathery green foliage on succulent stems are a gorgeous sight and are not meant to be resisted.

COLOUR KEY

1. Bright red
2. Hot pink
3. Violet
4. Racing green
5. Black

Slipping into pink

Inspiration can come from random colour combinations. This bright pink slipper brings out similar tones in the floral rug, showing how the choice of an accessory colour can influence the way we see a multi-coloured pattern. Our eyes seek out the matched colour and it becomes more visually important than others in the pattern.

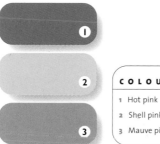

COLOUR KEY

1 Hot pink
2 Shell pink
3 Mauve pink

Exotic pink

This strong pink fabric embossed with a gold border and pattern motif was inspired by the beautiful saris worn by women in India. The hot pink originates from India, where the skill of manufacturing brilliantly coloured dyes pre-dates that of Western civilization by thousands of years.

COLOUR KEY

1 Hot pink
2 Golden yellow
3 Creamy yellow

passionate: **hot pink**

Some like it hot

Hot pink is a tropical colour most at home in brilliant sunshine, surrounded by other vibrant colours. Think of an Indian street scene with the women's saris a riot of clashing colours. Or South America, where woven textiles are coloured with natural dyes to produce the most brilliant range of colours, including a startlingly vibrant pink. Outside the tropics this colour is best suited for use in a room where there is limited natural daylight or where the room is mainly used in the evenings.

Perfect harmony

In this very feminine room the walls have been painted in the most brilliant shade of pink and then softened by using pink, white and lavender floral prints to diffuse the impact of the shocking pink. The same bright pink appears in all the prints so that the effect is entirely harmonious.

COLOUR KEY	
1 Hot pink	**1**
2 Pale lavender	**2**
3 Pale mauve pink	**3**

Pink shock

Hot pink hits you right between the eyes. Also called shocking pink, it is one of the most energetic colours you can buy in a can. Ten years ago the colour was impossible to find but now it is all the rage and most paint companies have produced a version of it. Children adore this colour; it is slightly wicked yet feels very positive and full of fun.

COLOUR KEY	
1 Bright red	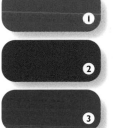
2 Bright purple	
3 Hot pink	

Tots to teens

The hot pink walls in this young girl's bedroom give it a funky style that is extremely popular at the moment. The accessories and soft furnishings are perfect for the under-tens and with a strong colour such as this one you always have the welcome option of giving it a more teenage look with new accessories and bed linen when the time comes.

COLOUR KEY	
1 Hot pink	
2 Warm pink	
3 Palest pink	

bright and lively

red

Red makes a powerful statement. It is the colour of lifeblood and the centre of a flame; of danger, anger, excitement, strength and fire. It is a powerful, alarming, extrovert colour. It is active, advancing and associated with physical activity, fire and passion. It can be aggressive, and has negative as well as positive associations.

The colour of revolution is also a colour of many different characters. It can look innocent with white in a gingham check; rustic with orange and brown; seductive as satin and velvet; cheerful in candy stripes or scrumptious as a bowl of cherries.

Red is a favourite colour in Western folk art, where the heart and the rose are popular motifs. In the Far East, red and gold are used in ceremonies.

Decorating with red needs careful consideration, but that is no reason to avoid it. Red is an attention-seeker, good for details and accessories. In a room used mainly at night, it will bring instant warmth and encourage sociability. Red stimulates the appetite, making it ideal for a dining room. It has traditionally been the colour of love and sex, so it may be perfect for a bedroom if sleeping is the last thing on your mind!

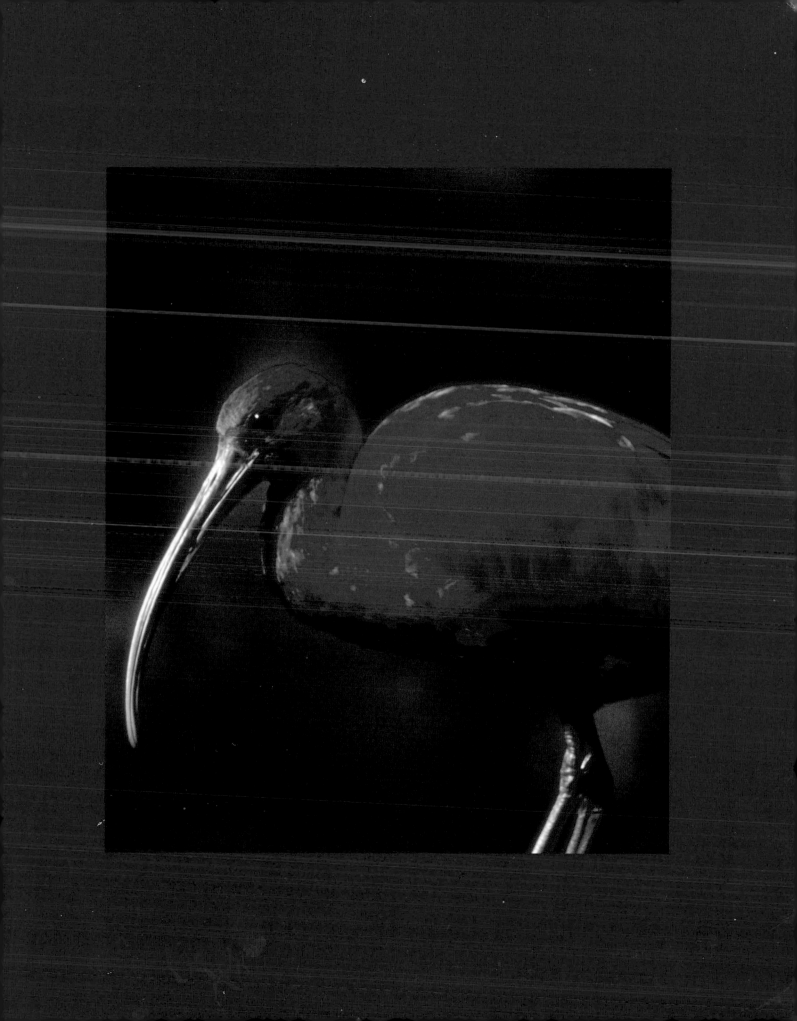

bright and lively: **red**

Attention seeker

Red gives out a signal and demands attention. We use red as a warning colour to indicate imminent danger but red in nature is more likely to suggest ripeness. Red can be a delicious colour and perhaps our decorating should be inspired by visions of a pile of red strawberries surrounded by a moat of cream. Red draws our eyes to it so that anything red will be the first thing we notice in a room. If this effect is too powerful for everyday use, save it for a special occasion when a vase of red flowers will give an instant impact.

Stunning sunset

A sunset like this is one of those precious moments when it is impossible to ignore the breathtaking truth that we are living on a planet in space warmed by the heat of a burning fireball. Everyday life in the Western world may conspire to have us forget this awe-inspiring fact, but somewhere out there, right now, the fiery red sun is setting in the inky blue sky.

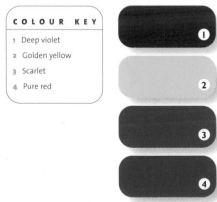

COLOUR KEY

1 Deep violet
2 Golden yellow
3 Scarlet
4 Pure red

1

2

3

4

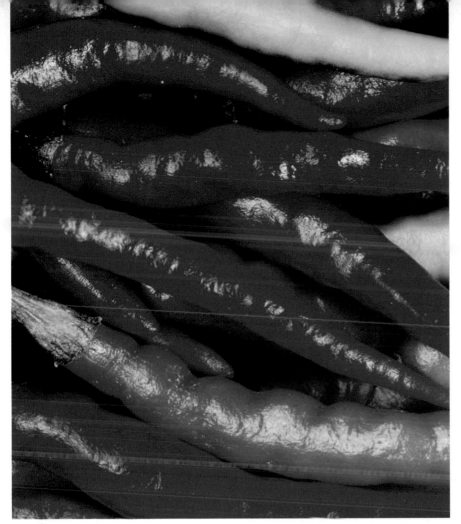

Chilli hot

The rich red of these chilli peppers provides a clue to their nature. These are burning pods of fire to be handled with care. The beauty of red chilli peppers has always been appreciated in countries like Mexico where they are strung up like bunting to dry in the sun. If your kitchen needs warming up, this could do the trick.

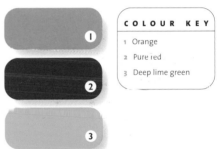

COLOUR KEY

1 Orange

2 Pure red

3 Deep lime green

Red alert

When birds wish to be noticed they smarten up their plumage and this scarlet ibis would be unmissable on land or in the air. A flash of a scarlet cushion, lampshade or bowl of bright red flowers will attract the eye in just the same way.

COLOUR KEY

1 Rich red

2 Hot pink

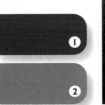

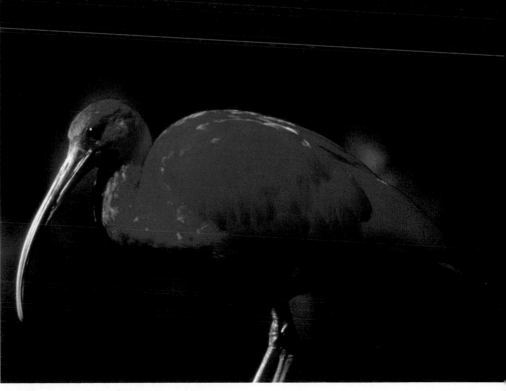

bright and lively: **red**

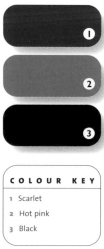

Going red

Decorating a room in red means you will be making a statement. Pure scarlet is red at its brightest, full of youth and fun. It's the red of chequered tablecloths, tomato-shaped ketchup dispensers and 1950s diner-style barstools. Red-brown has a more comforting effect in the form of the natural red of quarry-tiled floors and polished mahogany. Deep crimson red is richer and contains blues and browns to give it warm and cool aspects. It's a luxurious, sexy red that oozes relaxed comfort and confidence.

Red heat

Red, black and orange create a hot mood in this bar area. The burnt orange ceiling and reflective red varnished floor intensify the hot pink wall, making the area pulsate with vibrant colour. This is a sophisticated look, which says clearly that this is a place where the grown-ups come to play. The cane bar furniture is early 1960s in style, and the slatted wooden blinds cleverly keep up the room's temperature by implying the need for shade.

① ② ③

COLOUR KEY

1 Scarlet
2 Hot pink
3 Black

Cherry red

The red in this kitchen is the colour of ripe cherries. The gloss painted surface picks up all the irregularities in the old plaster and the shape of the wooden panels, while also reflecting the creamy yellow tiles and chrome chair. A deep red such as this benefits from a gloss finish, which has the effect of knocking it back where it would otherwise advance. This is a brave colour choice for a kitchen; it works well here because of the room's proportions and the light that floods in through the tall window. Keeping to just two strongly contrasting colours make a powerful statement.

COLOUR KEY

1 Cherry red
2 Pale pistachio
3 White

Night and day

Red is a highly stimulating colour, ideal for a home office where action is the name of the game. Working from home is convenient but you miss out on the transition travel period when you have time to adapt yourself from home to work mode. Red will signal the change-over in an instant. Red with cream is a more sophisticated colour combination than red and white, and with this cleverly concealed office-in-a-cupboard, the room could easily convert into an intimate dining area for the evenings.

COLOUR KEY

1 Rich red
2 Creamy white

stimulating
blue

Stimulating blue is cool, spatial and invigorating. Blue is associated with peace, masculinity, intuition, cleanliness, trust, authority and intelligence. In some shades blue is balancing, calming and rejuvenating, a colour with the power to replace excitement with tranquillity – perfect to come home to after a draining day at work.

Blue is the coldest colour in the landscape, and the one of distance. Blue absorbs light and will make a room appear considerably darker than it would if painted with a light-reflecting colour such as yellow.

Walls painted blue appear to recede, so put blue to work when space is at a premium. The eye perceives blue as having a blurred edge, so it is useful for softening hard edges in a room.

Bright blue and white are a crisp combination because white sharpens up blue edges, while blue makes white look cleaner and brighter. Indoors, this combination needs a shot of balancing orange or golden yellow to warm it up. Blue is good to use outdoors, providing a resting place for the eyes in bright sunshine. The shade beneath blue parasols looks the coolest and most inviting of all.

stimulating: **blue**

COLOUR PALETTE

Heavenly blue

Pure bright blue is a heavenly colour. It can freshen a space, making it feel cool and airy. It is a meditative colour, good for focusing the mind on higher things. Pale blue is soft, relaxing and gentle. Ultramarine is the deep intense blue of the night sky. Its depth can be disturbing and needs to be balanced with a warm, positive colour such as gold, yellow or orange. Blue mixes well with other colours, and the resulting shade may be interesting or unusual but it will never be unpleasant. Blue is the most popular colour.

Sky, sea and sand

The deep, almost Prussian, blue sky and turquoise sea set against white sands present an example of how to decorate on a grand scale. The yellow starfish in the foreground provides a welcome colour and textural contrast. To recreate this spatial effect in a room, make use of the receding quality of a deep blue with an advancing pale yellow.

COLOUR KEY

1 Prussian blue
2 Pale mint
3 Aqua
4 Peachy pink

Country fresh

One of the most stunning sights in early summer are the acres of brilliant yellow rapeseed flowers set against a clear blue sky. The sky looks bluer and surrounding green fields look greener under the influence of this brilliant yellow. A bright yellow throw, blind or table cloth can similarly brighten all the colours in a room.

COLOUR KEY

1 Deep pure blue
2 Primrose yellow
3 Bright leaf green

Shades of blue

The layered blues of this mountain scene have an intense unreal beauty. In the moments between day and night before the light fades, the blues in the landscape achieve their fullest intensity.

COLOUR KEY

1 Light blue
2 French blue
3 Prussian blue

stimulating: **blue**

COLOUR
PALETTE

Freshen up

Blue is the colour to reach for when a room needs refreshing. Blue can brighten and expand a room and a small area of blue can make a big difference. The spatial qualities of blue are invaluable and the colour gives the perception of a lower temperature, which makes it very useful for an office where it helps concentration and stimulates ideas. A blue kitchen will feel more comfortable when the heat is on and a blue bathroom will provide more refreshment than relaxation.

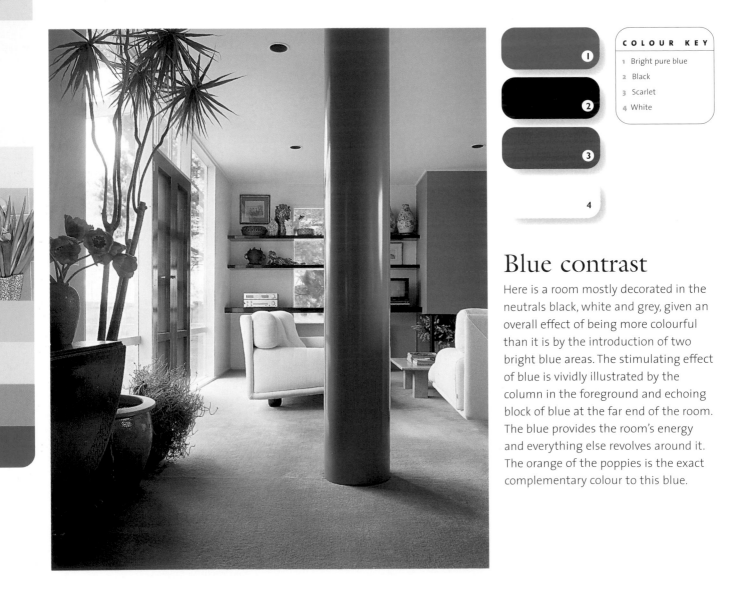

COLOUR KEY

1 Bright pure blue
2 Black
3 Scarlet
4 White

Blue contrast

Here is a room mostly decorated in the neutrals black, white and grey, given an overall effect of being more colourful than it is by the introduction of two bright blue areas. The stimulating effect of blue is vividly illustrated by the column in the foreground and echoing block of blue at the far end of the room. The blue provides the room's energy and everything else revolves around it. The orange of the poppies is the exact complementary colour to this blue.

Bright blue

This is the bright blue of the cloudless Mediterranean sky, the deep end of the swimming pool and the striped awnings outside a seaside café. Yellow and white look great beside it. Notice how the deep blue intensifies the colour and the yellow attracts the eye and provides relief from the intensity of the blue. When using a strong colour like this it is always important to introduce a small area of another equally bright colour to provide visual balance.

COLOUR KEY
1 Pure blue
2 Lemon
3 Deep lime

Soothing space

The wood panelling and beautiful window make this a very special space indeed. The simple table and two chairs in natural pale wood look especially inviting surrounded by this beautiful shade of blue. This is a place to sit, talk and share. The blue colour scheme would create a similar effect if used on the interior of a conservatory or porch area, where you are protected from the elements and have the sense of being inside yet outside.

COLOUR KEY
1 Ice blue
2 Soft aqua
3 Pale lavender

energising
orange

Energising orange is like the child in the family of colour. It is hugely attractive, positive and full of zing; sociable, direct, creative and secure. Orange is a warm, cheerful colour, symbolising prosperity, and both physical and mental energy. It is associated with brilliant autumn leaves against blue skies, the warmth of leaping flames and the pumpkin lanterns at Hallowe'en parties.

Orange is light-reflective and can considerably increase both the light and our perception of warmth in a room. It is a good choice for entrance halls and rooms where people gather to socialise. The freshest shade of orange is the colour of the skin of the ripe fruit, and contains all its promise of sunshine, sparkling good health and pleasure.

Bright orange can cause a sensory overload and needs balancing with a cool colour such as aqua, blue or green. The addition of white will remove most of orange's vivacious impact but none of its warmth, creating a more subtle, mellow colour. The Georgians used orange in their print rooms, it was all the rage in the 1920s and again in the 1970s, and orange is now back in fashion again.

energising: **orange**

COLOUR
PALETTE

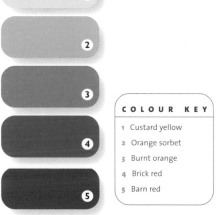

Outstanding orange

Burnt orange is one of the richest natural earth colours. It is versatile and can mix with other deep natural pigments, or be the focal point in a sophisticated minimalist room. Sharp orange is vivacious. It refuses to be taken seriously and is the one to choose for a witty retro-fashion statement. Pale orange is a creamy, mellow colour that is warm and welcoming. It feels hospitable and looks fabulous with its opposite number – icy blue. Pale orange's warmth matches the coolness of stainless steel, chrome and glass.

COLOUR KEY

1 Custard yellow
2 Orange sorbet
3 Burnt orange
4 Brick red
5 Barn red

Autumnal hues

Autumn does not last very long but during those weeks, especially if skies are blue, we see some of the most stunning colours that nature has to offer. The sun is low in the sky and the leaves are lit up at tree level. A deciduous New England woodland like this one has every shade of orange leaves, from pale yellow through to brilliant scarlet.

Hot and spicy

The spice colours of turmeric, paprika and cayenne are warm and earthy. The bright orange-yellow turmeric is ground from a root and cayenne is powdered, dried chilli peppers. These spices have been the most recent source of inspiration for paint colours in many shades of orange.

COLOUR KEY

1 Paprika
2 Pure orange

Sun over Africa

This extraordinary picture of children herding cattle in the African sunset reveals the scale of the dry, flat landscape, about to be plunged into darkness. The sun dominates life in the semi-desert, seeming larger and more brilliantly orange at sunset here than it is anywhere else on earth.

COLOUR KEY

1 Luminous yellow
2 Burnt orange
3 Bright red

energising: **orange**

Bold and brave

It comes as no surprise to find that orange is one of the favourite colours used by professional interior designers for living rooms and entrance halls. The colour gives a room fresh energy and it is a choice that requires a certain amount of bravado. A designer's job is to have that sort of confidence and they know that if they can influence a client to have orange the room will be a great success. Orange may look brash in the tin but it's great on walls and as soft furnishings.

Energetic orange

This is a good example of the way orange can work its magic in a room. The alcove shelving next to the fireplace here is functional and the objects on display are a very personal, homely collection with no co-ordinated style. It is the choice of broad orange and white striped fabric for the curtain that makes the room interesting by adding a ripple of colourful energy.

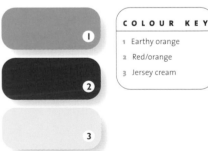

COLOUR KEY

1 Earthy orange
2 Red/orange
3 Jersey cream

A warm welcome

The use of inviting, welcoming orange in an entrance hall immediately gives out the message that the occupants of the house are warm, friendly, sociable people who care about their environment and their friends. There is a suggestion of opulence in the elegant display of objects on the desk and the stunning flowers dramatically reflected in the ornate mirror behind.

COLOUR KEY

1. Cinnamon
2. Rose red
3. Warm orange

Full of bravado

The bravado of using so much orange in one room is justified by the resultant warmth, energy and sense of security it provides. If you imagine this to be a cool basement apartment without any access to direct sunlight, then you will appreciate the power of colour to radiate heat. This is a literally brilliant treatment for a cool dark room.

COLOUR KEY

1. Sunflower yellow
2. Pale apricot
3. Pure orange
3. Deep orange

COLOUR PALETTE

serenity
purple

Being surrounded by lilac and purple is said to help us achieve serenity. But purple is a colour of contradictions – it also has strong associations with royalty and mourning. Purple is linked to creativity and is favoured by artists, musicians and those who tend towards an eccentric, bohemian lifestyle. It is believed to have a negative influence on people with susceptible temperaments, and those prone to depression should avoid it.

The colour ranges between blue and red, with blue-violet at one end and maroon at the other. Violet is the darkest and deepest colour of the spectrum. The more red a purple contains, the warmer and more comforting it becomes. Deep purples are too heavy for large areas, but are tremendous for adding depth, richness and colour accents to a room.

Pale lilacs, lavenders and violets have the opposite effect, and are excellent for walls and ceilings. Used in harmonious colour schemes, their effect is cool but comfortable, making them ideal for bedrooms and studies. In a room used for more sociable activities, the colours work best with warm contrasts, such as earthy oranges and deep yellows.

serenity: **purple**

Sumptuous purple

Royal purple is the colour of robes and pageantry. It is associated with wealth and luxury of the highest order. The look and feel of silk, velvet and satin are well-suited to purple. Violet is the deepest spectrum colour. Decorating with this colour indicates confidence with contemporary style. Lavender is a soft pale purple, which is infused with relaxing meditative powers. It can be masculine or feminine, and is enhanced by the proximity of blues and greens.

Lovely lilac

The lilac blossom is one of the first memorable garden scents of early summer. The flowers appear in so many shades of purple from almost white to the deepest rich violet, warm purple and pink. The leaves are pale yellow-green and glossy. Let nature inspire your colour choices.

1

2

3

COLOUR KEY

1 Cool pale lavender

2 Pinky mauve

3 Lilac

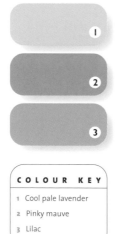

Night skies

Red sky at night produces wonderful colour effects as the sun sets over the blue sea. Purple waves are a rare and extraordinary sight. This depth and range of liquid colours would be impossible to replicate in paint, but the colours could be introduced using iridescent fabrics like moiré satin or silk.

COLOUR KEY

1 Dusky blue
2 Lilac
3 Pale aqua
4 Sand yellow

Lavender blue

A lavender field in full bloom presents one of the most attractive views of cultivated land. The bushes are grown in rows giving the effect of a very large purple quilt when seen from a distance. The smell is heavenly and should definitely be included to enhance the atmosphere as part of any lavender colour scheme.

COLOUR KEY

1 Deepest lavender
2 Bright apple green
3 Deep avocado green

serenity: **purple**

COLOUR
PALETTE

Purple trends

In Victorian times purple was the colour of mourning, and this association took a long time to wear off. It was in the Swinging Sixties that purple first became associated with youthful rebellion and rock 'n' roll. It graduated into mainstream fashion and decorating, usually in muted shades of aubergine. Purple is back on top of the adventurous decorator's list now, thanks to TV make-over programmes. It is a colour to use boldly to make a statement or in small amounts to add drama to a neutral colour scheme.

Stress relief

These walls have been treated with the most effective stress-busting colour of all. This deep lavender purple is associated with the mind's higher thoughts and meditations. If your office environment needs to be more focused and less frantic, then this is the colour to choose. The combination of deep colour for the walls, pale natural wooden furniture and an efficient open storage system gives the office a cool, contemporary look.

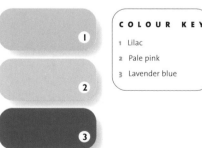

COLOUR KEY

1 Lilac
2 Pale pink
3 Lavender blue

Lilac echoes

The placing of one colour alongside another will always influence the way it looks. The colour of the bedroom walls here is picked up on the border of the bedlinen along with bands of soft aqua and pink. The white separates the colours ensuring that they remain pure and fresh.

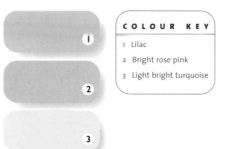

COLOUR KEY

1 Lilac
2 Bright rose pink
3 Light bright turquoise

Cool kitchen

This vast old kitchen with its high ceiling has been transformed in a contemporary homely style with a coat of lilac paint. The combination of lilac, cherry red and white with chrome and stainless steel gives the room a cool youthful style that mixes current fashion with 1950s revival. The colour is affected by its neighbours, looking pale near white and more magenta alongside the red. It appears most intense in the shaded areas where it deepens to a much richer shade of violet. Lilac is tremendously popular and the stores are filled with lilac accessories and soft furnishings.

COLOUR KEY

1 Lavender
2 Pale lilac
3 Deep salmon pink

sociable
yellow

Sociable yellow is a colour that makes us feel happy, warm and gregarious. Yellow glows and is light-reflecting, which makes it a very useful colour for rooms with a northerly aspect where its effect is one of instant sunshine. It is the brightest of the true colours and carries with it all the positive qualities of brilliance and light. Symbolically, yellow is associated with intellect, understanding and knowledge. Buddhist monks wear saffron yellow robes as a sign of their spiritual enlightenment. Yellow is strongly affected by the colours used alongside it – with black it is at its most luminous; with violet it looks hard; with orange it appears purer, and with green it radiates life and energy.

Yellow and blue can be an uncomfortable combination unless the shade of blue is softened with grey. Red and yellow are celebratory colours, full of fun and very bold. Use yellow in a large kitchen where meals are prepared and served – you will be guaranteed a lively atmosphere and good conversation at meal times. In a playroom it will encourage generosity and good behaviour, and in a work room it will encourage imagination, creativity and communication.

sociable: **yellow**

Shades of yellow

Sunshine yellow radiates warmth, confidence and goodwill. This effect is intensified and energised by a glossy reflective surface. Pale primrose yellow has a soft feminine character. Deep mustard yellow is heavy and rich, a match for powerful colours like scarlet and purple. Creamy custard yellow goes with everything – it is comforting, warm, friendly and unchallenging. Lemon yellow has a hint of sharp green in it, and brilliance but no warmth. Its coolness can impart an air of sophistication, especially when used with black.

Mellow yellow

Banana yellow can be tinged with green or dotted with brown. The banana itself is a pale, creamy yellow and it is the skin colour that grabs the attention. The colour has none of the brashness of golden yellow or coolness of citrus yellow. This must be the original mellow yellow.

COLOUR KEY

1 Deep orange
2 Golden yellow
3 Sharp yellow

Floral tones

The fragile perfection of yellow rose petals is not easy to capture with a paint colour. The outer petals are pale and translucent, while the closely furled inner petals have a richer, deeper colour. A fresh bunch of yellow roses will brighten any room.

COLOUR KEY

1 Jersey cream
2 Pale spring green
3 Golden yellow

Soft as down

Ducklings are a wonderfully pure, soft yellow. The downy texture allows the light to shine through the young feathers and reveal their delicacy and softness. To paint walls this softest shade of yellow, begin with a mid-tone of yellow as a base coat, then apply a pale yellow using a dry brush and random short strokes to imitate the texture. Keep the effect subtle and the brush strokes light.

COLOUR KEY

1 Orange-yellow
2 Lemon curd
3 Palest apricot

sociable: **yellow**

Convivial colour

Decorating a room yellow is like sending out an 'open house' invitation. This colour is associated with warmth, goodwill and sociability. It is very reflective and on a bright day will infuse a room with yellow light. Earthy yellow is warm and looks good in a farmhouse setting or a sophisticated living room, while primrose yellow is fresh and suits a light, airy contemporary style. Citrus yellow is the coolest shade with a lime green cast. It's sharp as a lemon and works well with bold contrasts. Each yellow is unique but all are convivial.

Instant sunshine

Corridors, passageways and entrance halls seldom have a natural light source – unless there is a skylight in the roof. These are areas to make the best use of yellow's light-enhancing properties. The brilliant yellow here has been used on the walls and ceiling to maximise its power, and the space vibrates with colour. The tulips are an extravagance, but the effect is dazzling.

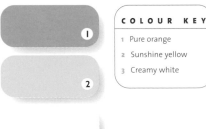

COLOUR KEY

1 Pure orange
2 Sunshine yellow
3 Creamy white

Colourful fun

Have some fun and celebrate the spectacular contrasts of shocking pink and bright yellow. Turquoise is the true complementary contrast here, but with an overpowering blast of colour like this it is difficult to pick out any one colour as dominant. The effect of yellow here is to brighten all the other colours.

COLOUR KEY

1 Hot pink
2 Scarlet
3 Pale peach
4 Citrus yellow

Attract a crowd

A kitchen this size will always be a social space where friends and family gather to chat over cups of coffee or to watch as the meal is prepared. The walls are a rich buttercup yellow that looks light and airy next to the solid natural wood units and granite work surface. The stainless steel and chrome add sparkle and the balancing colour is picked up with the large mauve pompom alliums. Painting a kitchen yellow will always attract company.

COLOUR KEY

1 Pistachio
2 Custard yellow
3 Bright mauve
4 Violet blue

COLOUR
PALETTE

harmonising
green

Green is the predominant colour of our planet from outer space. Green is the colour of youth, growth, ecology, relaxation, balance, recovery and optimism. It connects us to nature. Green soothes disturbed emotions and provides restful sleep, which makes it the ideal colour for a bedroom. It is a favourite colour in hospitals where its calming influence counteracts fear and trauma.

Green is the perfect foil for most other colours, but when using several greens together it is best to keep to light and dark tones of the same green. Sea green and olive, for instance, make a sickly combination, as do yellow-green and pine. If in doubt, search through a plant manual for the best green combinations – nature never gets it wrong.

Although green is a cool colour, it will not make a room feel cold so long as there are some warm contrasts. The lighter greens feel most youthful, refreshing and full of positive energy, just like new growth in springtime. They look good in a contemporary-style room with plum-purple and chocolate-brown. Olive, moss, lime and lichen are other unusual shades of green with a contemporary edge.

harmonising: **green**

Nature's colour

Sage is a soft green-grey which is very easy on the eye – a most restful, cool, meditative colour. Sage itself is the herb associated with wisdom and memory. Muddy green is thought to be depressing because of its associations with decay in nature, and lime green can induce feelings of nausea. Leaf green is the colour of new shoots, full of freshness, hope and energy. Pine green can be cold unless brightened with strong contrasts. A deep green looks good with burnt orange and cream.

Fern effects

This cool and shady forest scene is filled with green – some shades are so deep they appear as black. The five-fingered ferns in the foreground create a three-dimensional effect with their fresh light colour against the deep green background. This idea could be used on a wall with a receding dark green as a background and a light-infused yellow-green leaf stencil as a pattern.

COLOUR KEY
1 Forest green
2 Leaf green
3 Light leaf green

Fabulously fruity

The shine on the surface of a buffed green apple is always quite enticing and provides us with a clue as to how to make the most of this colour. A flat matt green will always be more of a pea soup than an apple colour. Lift the green with a reflective glossy varnish or provide shimmering accessories to lighten its mood.

COLOUR KEY

1 Apple green
2 Pale fern

Lush green

What could be greener than green frogs seen through a lush green leaf in the jungle? Using inspiration like this for your colour schemes is a lot more fun than choosing from a paint card. To create a luminous green like the leaf colour, apply a strong lemon yellow beneath a wash or glaze of fresh green. The yellow will illuminate the green from below.

COLOUR KEY

1 Tropical green
2 Yellow green
3 Light avocado

harmonising: **green**

Simple harmony

The 'green room' in a theatre is the place where actors relax before a performance, and although not always literally green any more, the colour association remains. To appreciate green's harmonising effect, think of a garden filled with many different coloured flowers. It is the green foliage around all these colours that allows them to blend so well together. Use green in the same way when you decorate, and you will find that the results are invariably harmonious.

Cool and calm

This small home office area has been created from a 'dead space' between rooms in a small apartment. Painting walls, ceiling and woodwork in shades of olive green has defined the space and made another room. The combination of olive tones and chrome are cool and contemporary and the area has a calm, concentrated atmosphere.

COLOUR KEY

1 Deep avocado
2 Olive
3 Fresh green
4 Silver grey

Mix and match

Here a background yellow provides a perfect foil for the many shades of green in this room. The rustic style of the green dresser is echoed in the handpainted wall pattern, which in turn resembles the open pattern of the metal furniture. Mixing greens can be difficult, but here it has been successfully achieved by limiting the room palette to just two harmonious colours.

COLOUR KEY

1 Light apple green
2 Mustard yellow
3 Yellow-green

Good companions

Green can be a difficult colour to match, but when brown is used alongside it the task is made easier. Brown is green's companion in nature, and it has a mellowing effect, easing out the minor differences in tone and intensity of two shades of green. Here the boldness of the wallpaper design is balanced by the elegant simplicity of the chairs and the splendid cactus centrepiece.

COLOUR KEY

1 Pale sage
2 Deep avocado
3 Barn red
4 Brick red

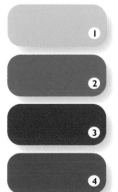

comforting
brown

Comforting brown is the colour of so many of the good things in life – polished wood, leather, crumbly earth, dogs and horses, freshly baked bread, coffee beans, pebbles in a stream, bowls filled with nuts and – perhaps best of all – chocolate.

It is a colour of great variations, but is always warm, whether tinged with red, green or yellow. Brown appears somewhere in most rooms as the colour of polished wood, but is often not credited as being a part of the colour scheme. Brown has occasionally been the height of decorating fashion – the Victorians, especially the Arts and Crafts movement, used it a lot for wallpaper, fabric and carpet patterns; it dominated homes in the 1940s, in a very drab way during the war years. In the 1970s, orange and brown was the hippest combination, and right now brown is back in fashion as a part of the natural palette.

Use dark brown in an eco-style room with soft sap green, taupe and olive; or mix contemporary dark wooden furniture with pale jade and deep plum walls. Deep chocolate brown and cream striped walls look delicious in a dining room, and red-brown floor tiles infuse a kitchen with warmth.

comforting: **brown**

Nature and nurture

Brown is the colour of the earth, rocks, roots and tree trunks. We associate brown with stability, comfort, warmth and nurture. The natural browns around us vary a great deal, but paint charts usually offer little choice. The best way to get the brown you want is to have a colour specially mixed. Your colour match could be anything from driftwood to a mushroom. A flat brown looks better than one with a sheen and the colour is more suited to an opaque fabric with some texture than a sheer fabric.

Feel-good

Chocolate contains a unique blend of feel-good chemicals which most of us find difficult to resist. Although the texture and delicious aroma present a problem, the warm colour of chocolate can translate into wall, floor and furnishing colours to give a similarly comforting effect.

COLOUR KEY

1 Rich brown
2 Brick red
3 Copper brown

Back to nature

The pine cone is one of mother nature's designer objects that falls from the trees and begs to be put on display in our homes. Pine cones are perfectly formed and have a fresh forest scent. They are rich in natural oils, which deepen their colour, and they fade to become paler as they dry out. A display of pine cones in a basket or pot creates a sculptural focal point in a room, especially when the room's colour scheme is inspired by nature.

COLOUR KEY

1 Chocolate
2 Deep rose
3 Soft grey

Urban chic

The colour of coffee beans is a sharper, fresher, redder brown than cocoa. At its purest it is lively and exciting but like the drink it becomes more mellow when diluted with white to a creamy latte shade. This is a sophisticated urban brown.

COLOUR KEY

1 Mahogany
2 Dusky rose
3 Dark chocolate

comforting: **brown**

Brown is back

Brown is always to be seen in wooden objects, floors, doors and furniture, but as a decorating colour it is either the height of fashion or not used at all. It was huge in the 1970s when everything from bathroom suites to sheets, carpets and curtains was brown. It became ubiquitous and was forced into hibernation for two decades, but now it's back. It fits well with the popular natural decorating style. It looks good with khaki greens and creams and also bright tropical colours and cool shades of lilac and turquoise.

Calm and neutral

The cool suede-look wall is actually a sand finish painted in a soft shade of mushroom brown, creating the perfect background for the contemporary bedroom furniture. The pale curved and polished wood presents an interesting textural contrast to the roughened wall and the overall effect is very calm, neutral and natural.

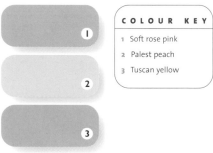

COLOUR KEY

1 Soft rose pink
2 Palest peach
3 Tuscan yellow

Textural delight

Coffee-brown walls in this stylish kitchen are a deliciously textured background for the stained wooden fitted kitchen. The room features many shades of brown with an interesting mixture of brickwork, beams and natural wooden floorboards. Everything co-ordinates, yet the brown does not overpower owing to the textural interest and superb natural light.

COLOUR KEY

1 Dusky pink
2 Shell pink
3 Coffee brown

Tasteful tones

This elegantly proportioned room is blessed with a good natural light source and fine floorboards. Chocolate brown is a very sophisticated colour choice as a background to this room where every object confirms the owners' good taste and design sense. The rich warm polished pine floor forms a harmonising base for the colonial style cane and polished wooden furniture. The rich brown walls manage to create a sense of intimacy in a very large room.

COLOUR KEY

1 Bitter chocolate
2 Palest lilac
3 Creamy custard

sophistication
black and white

Black and white present such a strong contrast that they are used over large areas only by the very brave or those wanting to make a grand statement. The Jazz era of the 1920s was typified by everything black and white, and rooms were furnished for parties and posing. Black and white next appeared in the late 1950s and early 1960s, when artists painted their studios white to reflect the light, and youth culture adopted the style for their homes. This style is still as cool as ever.

The dramatic effect of black and white can be stark and cold unless handled with sensitivity. The secret of success is to have lots of colourful ethnic artifacts and interesting paintings to display against the pure white background.

Japanese style is gaining popularity in the West and, although the black used is often a very dark brown and the white has the slightly yellow cast of unbleached paper, the style is one of stark contrasts. The Japanese have perfected the art of minimalism and use very few pieces of exquisitely shaped furniture whose shape is revealed by the sharp contrasts between the dark objects and their light background.

Artistic balance

This bathroom feels light, airy and balanced with heavy black low down and pure light-reflecting white everywhere else. Black is the best choice for blending shapes and masking unwanted features such as exposed pipework. Here black and white have been used to make a very simple but artistic style statement.

COLOUR KEY

1 Black
2 Bright French blue
3 White

Simply striking

Black and white is a sophisticated choice for a kitchen where any colour deviation will become the centre of attention. Food packaging is designed to be noticed and has no place here, so everything is hidden behind closed doors. White walls and units dominate, with black defining the space. Shape becomes very important when strong contrasts are used, because all edges are hard. A background like this provides a great opportunity to make bold but temporary colour statements. A bowl of oranges or a plate of red peppers would be sure to make an impact.

COLOUR KEY

1 Black
2 White
3 Hot orange

metallics
gold

Gold is the most glamorous metallic colour, designed to catch the eye as well as to highlight and frame in decorative schemes. The fashion for gold comes and goes. Much European furniture from the 16th century onwards was gilded, and during the Regency or Empire period it was used as decoration on black ebony furniture. Chinese lacquered furniture in red and black with fine gold filigree patterns influenced artists and designers in the late Victorian era.

In the 1980s gold made a big comeback in interior decorating, and this time it was more sassy than classy.

Gold, white leather, mirror tiles, deep shagpile carpets and perhaps a tented ceiling sent out all the right signals, but the look was never meant to last.

In the contemporary home gold is most likely to appear as part of an ethnic-inspired colour scheme such as one from India, Thailand or Morocco, where fabrics and accessories are often patterned with gold.

A magical array of modern products creates very convincing shades of gold. The most important thing about gold is that it gleams by day and sparkles in candlelight and, being fake, it should not take itself too seriously.

Thai style

Thailand has a lush green landscape peppered with temples and golden Buddhas. The mixture of green and gold evokes the countryside; the saffron, deep orange and gold are the traditional temple colours and brilliant colour mixtures of jade, fuchsia, electric blue and gold are the colours people wear on the street.

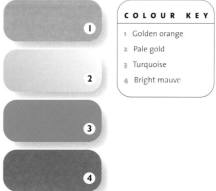

COLOUR KEY

1 Golden orange
2 Pale gold
3 Turquoise
4 Bright mauve

Going for gold

When you want to make a big impact, choose gold. Inspired by the multi-coloured sofa, this room has been painted a vibrant blue with a golden yellow ceiling and burnt orange floor. Faced with this riot of colour, the angelic finishing touch is a stroke of brilliance with the lustre of pure gold.

COLOUR KEY

1 Gold
2 Lavender blue
3 Burnt orange

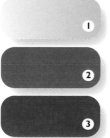

metallics
silver

Silver is the moon's colour and it is thought, by association, to have a balancing, feminine influence on us. It flatters most other colours and is very easy to fit into a colour scheme. Silver is cool and sharp with a reflective mirrored surface that picks up surrounding colours. It is the colour of pewter, stainless steel, zinc, tin, chrome, aluminium and galvanised iron. In the past decade, since the arrival of the industrial style, many of these silver metals have been making a big impact on home decorating.

Silver is most likely to dominate in the kitchen, where 'catering style' demands professional style cooking ranges, stainless steel work surfaces, sinks and appliances. Chrome is popular for items such as kettles, toasters and food mixers.

Elsewhere, painted silver walls look good with colours such as purple, lilac, cool blues and rosy pink and with soft fabric textures like velvet and silk that share silver's reflective qualities.

Whether you prefer the dull deep tones of pewter; the soft sheen of stainless steel, the sparkle of shimmering silver leaf or the mirror brightness of chrome, it is time to introduce some silver in your home.

Industrial chic

This metal platform provides a sturdy sleep area in a loft-style apartment. The look is very popular but can be hard and cold to live with. As an alternative, there are now several impressive brands of water-based metallic paints that can be used to give a tired wooden platform bed a new industrial chic style. Accessories really make a style like this and there are plenty of chairs, lamps, mirrors and bins around that will help to pull the look together.

COLOUR KEY

1 Silver
2 Black
3 Cream

Reflected glory

Chrome and stainless steel pick up all the light and colour in a room while retaining their own distinctive colour. These materials are mostly used for utility objects, like these espresso machines and teapots. The shelf arrangement is practical and decorative and sets the style of the room.

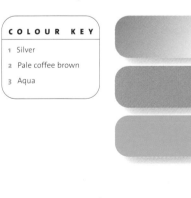

COLOUR KEY

1 Silver
2 Pale coffee brown
3 Aqua

The introduction of texture changes the appearance of a colour. The highs and lows of the pattern bring an element of light and shade to the wall, and provide another level of visual interest. Until recently texture, in the form of thick wallpaper or swirling plaster patterns, was often used only to conceal structural problems, but now applied texture has emerged as a serious contender in contemporary-style decoration. Paint effects are also making a comeback, being used to create areas of textural contrast or to add all-over wall patterns in a linen, denim or damask effect.

Introduction

 In this chapter we explore texture and the ways it can be used to add depth to a decorating scheme and enhance the impact of the colours. Several step-by-step projects are included that will help add character to a new house. There are contemporary ideas for white and very pale rooms where the main colour theme is neutrality. There is a matt and glossy white on white stencilling project and one showing how to make the softest floor cushion with a cover made from a baby's cot blanket or fleece fabric.

ECO PALETTE

The eco palette consists of a range of earthy, muddy and dull green colours, which look wonderful when combined with natural fabrics and materials such as linens, cottons, rush matting and earthenware. We include a project that uses two different muddy pale browns to decorate a wall and another that shows you how to make dramatic drapes with unbleached calico and a staple gun. Liming wax is used to transform an old chair by restoring the beauty of the grain, and some very basic upholstery skills are used to re-cover the seat pad with tactile suede.

COLOUR CONTRASTS

Colour contrasts can be used to create some dramatic special effects but colour can also be used in a practical sense to alter visually the proportions of a room or to disguise features that we would prefer not to see. One project in this section shows how to use two vibrantly contrasting complementary colours to create an energetic wall effect. There is also a project showing how to use a simple shadow to create a three-dimensional box and another that borrows a pattern from patchwork quilting to create the illusion of a three-dimensional frieze running around the room.

LEFT **Natural wood flooring, a sheepskin rug and a bowl of vibrantly coloured oranges – a simple combination, but very pleasing to the eye.**

bright tissue paper to a pasted wall area. This is a fairly time-consuming project and is best suited to a small area such as an alcove. Another project has an eco theme showing how to apply cane or bamboo screening to the lower half of a wall. The cane or bamboo can either be left natural and varnished to a high sheen or painted to match the wall and accentuate the change in texture.

The final project in this section creates a soft comfort zone for a small child but could also be used to define a sleeping area in a bedsitting room. This project uses brightly coloured fleece fabric to make cool hard walls softer and more appealing.

WALL COVERINGS

Textured wall coverings are back in fashion after a very long absence, although the new patterns lean more towards 1970s geometric patterns than the original Victorian styles.

Natural materials, such as split bamboo, raffia, hemp and linen, provide the textural contrasts that are so important when you are using the neutral palette, and in addition there are imitation pressed steel patterns that will give a room an industrial look at the swish of a pasting brush.

WALL TEXTURES

The last three projects in this section of the book all deal with the challenge of changing wall textures, and three different materials are used to this end.

One project produces a random patchwork of colour that is created by applying torn and creased pieces of

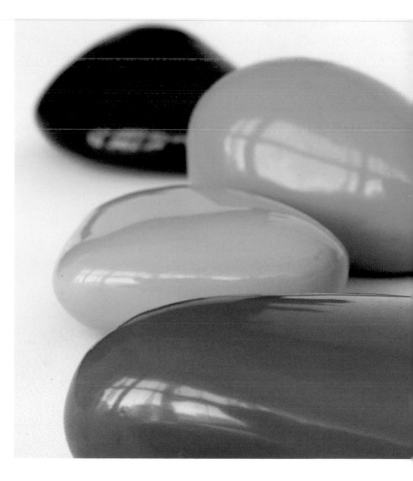

RIGHT **Stone can add interesting texture to any room, whether highly polished and brightly coloured, or rougher and neutrally coloured.**

Texture

 The way we choose and combine different textures for decorating is as much affected by trends as by our colour choices. Felt, once used only as a protective barrier, underlay or cushioning under a more decorative fabric, now makes a serious fashion statement. Plastic used to be seen as horrible, tacky and cheap, but now it's the last word in urban chic. Concrete was strictly functional and best kept hidden until minimalists rediscovered its potential. Brightly coloured laminated worktops are now back in demand.

ABOVE **The way to use texture in a neutral palette is to set different weaves, stripes or smooth surfaces against each other. Here we have a corded carpet on the horizontal, with woven baskets on the diagonal to create an energetic textural contrast. The papier-mâché bowl breaks up the pattern and the even smoother stick adds a tactile finishing touch.**

CREATING INTEREST

Texture does not only replace colour – it can also be used exclusively for its tactile and visual qualities. The roughness, smoothness or spikiness of a surface describes its texture. There are endless variations and combinations of textures that can be brought into play to make the home environment a more interesting and stimulating place.

Houses are being built faster than ever these days, with less attention to detail, and wherever we live most of us do it in an arrangement of smooth-sided, interconnecting box shapes. Old houses are more likely to have interesting architectural features to break up the monotony of plain walls, such as plaster mouldings, high skirting boards, and dado and picture rails. In their absence, there are many wall coverings and specialist paints that can be used to add interest. Anaglypta is a wall texture that has been around for more than a hundred years. The raised patterns were often used in heavy-duty areas such as hallways and staircases, where they adhered with such ferocity that any attempt to remove them brought most of the plaster off the wall as well. The original company still produces textured wall coverings, and has new ranges that look perfect in contemporary rooms. A more recent arrival is a wallpaper range with a raised texture in metallic finishes, which mimics aluminium flooring. It makes the full industrial look much more accessible and less of a permanent commitment, as the surfaces can be painted over with ordinary emulsion paint. Other new textures in wallpaper are a mixture of rough and smooth geometric patterns, widely spaced medallion shapes and ranges of natural materials such as bamboo, linen or woven reed panels. Cork is another warm, interesting natural texture due for a comeback – it looks good with dark wood, leather and chrome furniture in sculptural modern shapes, and as a bonus it provides excellent noise insulation.

One of the reasons that the colours we choose from a paint chart surprise us by looking different on our walls is that any variation in texture will introduce elements of light and shade to alter the regularity of the colour. Clever use of texture can really add depth to a colour scheme, making the difference between an ordinary and an exceptional room.

Our eyes are constantly travelling over surfaces and colours to evaluate and balance what we see. Clever interior designers understand this, and provide interest and relaxation in equal measures, making a room as visually satisfying and comfortable as possible.

ABOVE **This bathroom has an enamelled iron bath with bright chrome taps and wood panelling on the walls. The starfish, shells, sponges and pebbles effectively recreate a sense of the shoreline.**

FAMILIAR TEXTURES

Some of the instantly familiar textures used in the home include: leather • suede • linen • cotton • wool • rattan • paper • rubber • corrugated cardboard • silk • velvet • wood • slate • glass • stone • shell • glazed and unglazed ceramics • cork • marble • PVC • fleece • fake fur • hard plastic • stainless steel • wire mesh • concrete • chrome • rough and smooth wood • foam • feathers • bamboo

LEFT **Slate grey walls with an extreme rustic finish have the potential to look dark and gloomy, but the juxtapostion of a fine wooden table gives a stunningly sophisticated effect. The lilac-glazed ceramic bowl and the high shine of the green apples add two more textures to this very intriguing environment.**

Paint effects

Paint effects have come a long way in recent years – not only do contemporary paint effects look better, but successful application is also a lot easier to achieve. The big paint companies have all produced ranges of special effect products, which are easy to use and guarantee good results. There is a textured paint to make new walls look like those of an old farmhouse. There are shiny, metallic paints that simulate hard metal, and there are even textile finishes to make your walls look like faded denim jeans.

EASY EFFECTS

Paint effects are fun, and there are several that require no specialist training.

WOODGRAINING AND DRAGGING

Essentially woodgraining and dragging are the same kinds of effect; they are both created by dragging a dry paintbrush through an oil-based glaze in the direction of the woodgrain. The difference is that in woodgraining you can create effects beyond that of imitating the pattern of the grain.

STENCILLING AND SPONGING

It comes as no surprise that stencilling is staging a comeback, because it is the easiest and least expensive way of applying a pattern. Everyone can cut a simple stencil, and there are thousands of more complex designs on the market. Stencilling is something most of us tackle as children but feel wary of trying on the walls. The first secret of stencilling success is using a removable spray adhesive on the back of the stencil so that it sticks to the wall as you paint. The second one is

ABOVE, LEFT **Woodgraining: you can use a graining comb to make attractive patterns by dragging the comb through an oil-based glaze.**

LEFT **A denim effect wall finish is a soft blue finish available in kit form. The wall is first coated in a pale blue, then rollered over in a denim blue glaze, which is dragged with a long-haired brush.**

RIGHT **Stencil cutting is easier if you stick the pattern onto the card or plastic with a removable spray. Use a very sharp craft knife, inserting the point and cutting away from any corners. Protect the work surface with a cutting mat or cardboard.**

BELOW **Sponging can be done with a natural sponge and paint should be applied quite sparingly. Here a contrasting colour is used to demonstrate the technique and a subtler effect can be achieved with a softer combination of colours. Rotate the sponge as you work to avoid a repetitious pattern.**

to dip your brush in the paint then wipe it on kitchen paper to remove all the moist paint and just leave a dry coating of colour. You can always apply more colour, but too much will cause blobbing and runs. The same rule applies to sponging, when paint should be applied with a light touch. The textured finishes are applied as a thick coating of plaster-based paint, which is then worked on with a brush, comb or sponge to score into the surface and lift some of the coating.

ABOVE **Use a comb or piece of plastic cut to size to create a pattern. This can simply be directional or geometric as here, with one square vertical one horizontal, or you could design your own effect.**

RIGHT **A sponge dabbed onto a textured base will create a simple raised pattern. This can look good in a rustic-style room, and can also be re-painted with a foam roller.**

FAR RIGHT **Roll a set of vertical stripes onto the wall from bottom to top and then paint a set of horizontal stripes in another colour with a roller to create this check effect.**

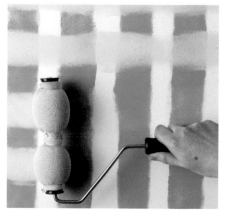

Shades of white

White comes in a great many subtle variations of colour and tone. Just one white standing alone is easily described. It is simply – white. A selection of whites seen together reveal that tones of white can be warm, cool, dull, bright, old, faded, blue, brown and many more possibilities besides. Brilliant white is the most reflective of all of the whites, and can be hard and dazzling when compared with a colour such as bone white, which is warm, soft and natural, or blue white, which is fresh and cool.

COLOUR PALETTE

The many white variations that we can now buy as named paint colours have been created to meet the demand for colour-free decorating schemes based on the idea of a 'pure' style. Colour and synthetics have no place in this white world, only natural fabrics and materials in a variety of white textures used together to create a harmonious, peaceful environment. The only acceptable colour here is the natural wood used for furniture and flooring, or the living green leaves of an indoor plant. It may sound like an impossible dream, but if the style is used in just one room it is simplicity itself. A bedroom or bathroom will be easiest, but good storage is essential because colourful clutter will ruin the effect.

Bedroom sanctuary

Use a chalky white distemper paint for the walls. Floors can be sanded and polished if the wood is pale, otherwise floorboards can be painted white. Scattered sheepskins or white flokati rugs are the perfect way to create islands of warmth on wooden floors, and make the most deliciously soft bedside rugs. Sheer, floaty white curtain panels, white

wooden shutters or natural linen blinds are all suitable for windows – much depends upon the aspect and the shape of your windows. Almost any style of furniture, old or new, can be used, so long as all fabrics are natural. An ordinary bed can be transformed into a four-poster by building a simple wooden frame surround and draping it with white muslin tab-topped curtains.

Bathroom sanctuary

This could be achieved with the most basic DIY toolkit and skills.

If your bathroom suite is white then you are already halfway there, and white-painted wood panelling or white tiles and towels are all you need. Textural contrasts will make the room look more interesting – matt for woodwork, gleaming tiles, polished chrome and folded fluffy towels. Flooring could be a good white marble-effect vinyl, or pale grey and white checks with white cotton-twist rugs. Frosted windows with a slight green tint will add extra freshness to a bathroom, and a pretty voile curtain panel will add a softening touch. If any colour is used, stick to the very palest shades of grey, fawn or aqua.

PROJECT
White on white stencil effect

YOU WILL NEED:

Two shades of white paint with contrasting finishes (such as satin and chalky finish)

Stencil material

A photocopy of the pattern

Spraymount

Craft knife

Broad stencil brush

Cloth

Plumb line (optional)

Spirit level (optional)

COLOUR KEY

1 Creamy white

2 Off-white

3 Peach white

The idea is to stencil a pattern of contrasting textures, which can either be rough/smooth, chalky/glossy or matt/glitter. The pattern is based on a geometric shape that is easy to enlarge and cut out. It can be stencilled in a regular grid pattern, or used randomly for a more casual effect.

A compromise between the two is best for large areas, moving a plumb line along a wall at regular intervals as a guide and stencilling in a half-drop pattern. Decide on the distance between the motifs, and stagger the rows so that in each alternate row the first motif falls halfway between those in the row before.

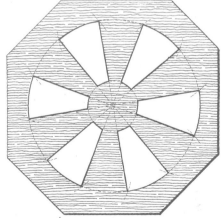

TEMPLATE

This pattern can either be constructed using a compass and a ruler or, simpler still, make a photocopied enlargement of this diagram to the size of your choice.

HOW TO DO IT

Stencilling a grid of bold shapes on the wall is simple and will give a very contemporary look to any room. To divide a wall into a grid use a plumb line to mark the verticals and a ruler with a spirit level for the horizontals.

STEP 1 Enlarge the pattern and apply a light drift of Spraymount to the back. Stick it onto a sheet of stencil card or mylar (the clear plastic stencil material).

STEP 2 Cut out the pattern with a craft knife, always cutting away from the corners towards the middle.

STEP 3 Paint the wall with the matt white paint and leave till bone dry.

STEP 4 Spray the back of the stencil with Spraymount and set aside. It should dry to a tacky finish that will stick to the wall when you are stencilling but be easily removed without leaving any sticky residue.

STEP 5 Place the stencil on the wall and use the chalky paint undiluted, applying a generous coating through the stencil with a broad stencil brush.

STEP 6 Lift the stencil and wipe the edges before repositioning it.

PROJECT
Floor cushion

YOU WILL NEED:

A foam/feather or polystyrene bead floor-cushion pad (low budget suggestion: buy a cheap floor cushion and re-cover it, or make a calico liner and fill it with a pair of old pillows).

A creamy white cot blanket or 1 metre (1 yard) fleece fabric

Scissors

Sewing machine

Iron

Cloth

Beige tapestry wool and a large needle for finishing in blanket stitch

White thread

In the white on white style, the floor is very much a part of the decorating scheme. Floor cushions are comfortable for lazing about on the floor. The project is simple and relies upon finding an interesting textured fabric and a trimming. The cushion cover in the project can be made from a cot blanket, which is the perfect shape as well as being wonderfully soft and inviting, or use one metre (yard) of fleece fabric. The cover is made in the most basic way, being machined on three sides and slip-stitched closed with the cushion pad inside. The blanket stitching suits the material perfectly.

COLOUR PALETTE

1

2

3

COLOUR KEY

1 Blue white

2 Cool white

3 Cream

HOW TO DO IT

This project is quick and easy, requiring only the most basic cutting out and sewing skills. The result is a smart and wonderfully soft floor cushion.

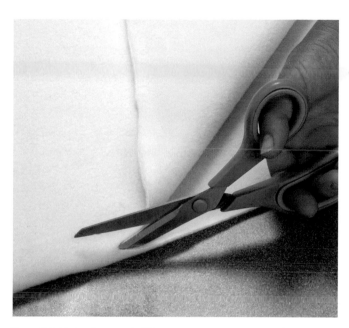

STEP 1 Fold the fleece in half lengthways and cut it to make two equal sized pieces.

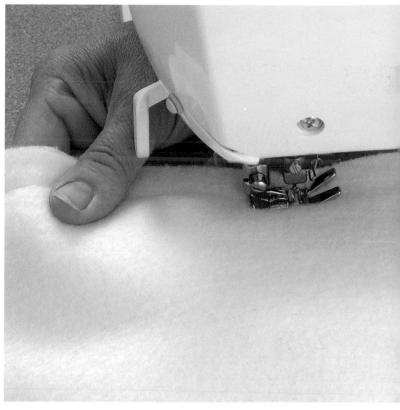

STEP 2 Cut off any edgings (which may be simple stitched folds or satin). Lay the two pieces on top of each other and stitch them together on three sides, 20mm (¾in) in from the edge.

STEP 3 Snip across the corners, then turn the other way out to conceal the seams and press flat, using a damp cloth to protect the fleece surface from the direct heat.

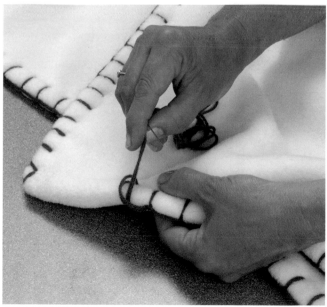

STEP 4 Thread the large needle with tapestry wool and sew a large blanket stitch on the three closed sides. Put the cushion pad inside and slip stitch to close the open end. Continue the blanket stitch along this seam.

Neutrals

The term 'neutral' applies to a range of indistinct tones and shades derived from mixtures of black and white with brown, grey, or sometimes with lesser amounts of muddy green, yellow or blue. A neutral colour scheme might be based around soft blue-toned grey or pale khaki brown, but whatever the slight colour cast, there will always be a high proportion of white. The neutrals are usually taken from the colour of a natural material such as parchment, sand, stone or marble, and work well with natural textures and materials.

A neutral colour scheme does not have to omit colour altogether, but the proportion of any other colours used should be small enough so as not to override its basic neutrality. Pattern is one way that a colour can be used without overpowering a scheme intended to be seen as neutral. This will work particularly well if the pattern combines the predominant neutral and a colour.

A colour scheme based around a single neutral does not have to look monotonous if an interesting mixture of tones and textures is used.

Sophisticated beige

A mid-beige vinyl silk paint on walls, with a dead flat darker mushroom beige on all woodwork and an almost white ceiling, does not sound all that thrilling. But add rough woven matting flooring, a large brown and white cowhide rug, loose weave drapes and a slatted wooden blind, a pale linen covered sofa with dark beige suede cushions and a mohair throw, and the room has become the epitome of contemporary sophistication. The same theory can be applied to any neutral decorating scheme.

Tranquil haven

A neutral colour scheme is superbly restful on the eyes. If you spend your days in an industrial environment or in the heart of a busy city, then this sort of room will be a haven of tranquillity at the end of the day. If a room is mainly used in the daytime, a pale neutral scheme will make the most of any natural light, which can be filtered using sheer muslin panels over the windows.

If a room is inclined to feel cold, make your selection from the warmer neutrals with yellowish tones, like cream, sand and pale straw. They look very good with pale greys or grey-greens. The cooler stone greys can be warmed up by the inclusion of a pinky beige.

Neutral backgrounds may be safe, but they certainly don't have to be dull or boring. A room painted in tones of stone grey on walls, ceiling and floor is like a vessel waiting to be filled. Strong colour statements can be saved for soft furnishings, contemporary furniture, paintings and dramatic lighting, even flower arrangements. Imagine the grey room with purple floor length curtains, leather and chrome classic chairs, a red sofa, a row of coloured neon tubes and a giant cactus plant.

PROJECT
Calico drapes

YOU WILL NEED:

Unbleached calico,
wide enough for two
curtains to cover the
window – measure
from floor to ceiling
and multiply by four
(this is to allow for a
generous draped
heading and some
billowing of the
curtains onto
the floor)

Staple gun
and staples

Iron-on bonding
tape or double-sided
tape for hems

Step ladder

Tie-back hooks

This is a project for those who enjoy a touch of drama with their decorating. It requires no sewing; it can be managed without a pin or a pair of scissors – but you'll need another pair of hands and a stepladder.

It is an unconventional but effective and economical way to drape a large window. The idea is simple enough – to use a single, long length of unbleached calico as two curtains and a draped heading, which is attached to the window frame using a staple gun.

If there is no wooden window frame, a batten fixed above the window would serve the same purpose.

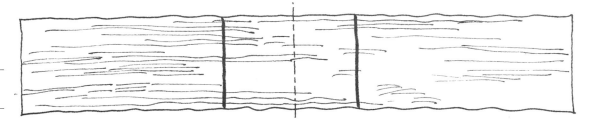

TEMPLATE

Divide the length of fabric in half and mark the centre line (above). Measure the window width; transfer the measurement to the fabric, the centre line running down the middle. Hold the length of fabric up to the batten and staple the two corners of the first marked line to the batten (above). Pleat (see opposite).

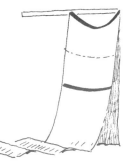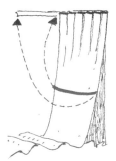

With one side pleated and stapled, pick up the length at the second marked line on the far edge and staple it up to the end of the batten (above, right). Staple the near edge to meet the first drop. Curtains are tied back during the day.

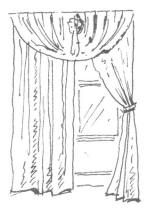

COLOUR KEY

1 Dusky blue
2 Maize
3 Hemp
4 Warm grey

HOW TO DO IT

This is such a stunning window treatment and much easier to do than to explain! It's like riding a bicycle – once learned never forgotten.

STEP 1 Hem one raw edge, and with a generous amount of this end resting on the floor on the left side of the window, take the rest of the fabric up the ladder with you. Line the fabric up with the top of the window frame and fold it over, allowing the excess to drop. Staple the fabric to the frame to overlap the centre of the window frame by 25mm (1in), then staple the other side to the window frame on the left. Much will depend on the type of window frame, but aim to conceal the top of the frame under the fabric.

STEP 2 If the fabric's width is much greater than half the window, then you will need to pleat the curtain. To do this, find the middle and staple it to the middle of the frame. Do the same again on each side of it, and then again, until all the slack is taken up in evenly stapled pleats. Now move the ladder to the other side of the window.

STEP 3 Drape the length of fabric across the top of the window until you reach the right edge of the frame. The line between the corners should fall in a gentle curve (see diagram). Now twist the fabric over, taking the right edge under the drape and into the centre, so that the rest of it falls to make the second curtain. Staple this right side curtain, pleating across the top in the same way as the left side.

STEP 4 Finish off the draped heading by gathering up and stapling the fabric in the middle, so that it falls in even drapes. Make sure that all the staples are concealed by the folds of fabric. Finally, fix tieback hooks into the sides of the window frame so that the curtains can be gathered up and tied back during the day.

PROJECT
Two-tone neutral wall

YOU WILL NEED:

Decorator's
masking tape

Set square

Long rule with a
spirit level

Pencil

Paint roller and tray

Paintbrush
(50mm/2in)

Two shades of
khaki beige

This project will be most useful for use in boxy rooms that have no interesting features to pick out. The idea is to create energy and interest by painting a wall in two harmonious tones of khaki beige. The two colours meet with a zigzag line at the height most complementary to the shape of the room. In a tall room keep the line in a low position, in a short one move it up, and in a long thin room it might be best to divide the wall vertically, with two thirds of the wall painted in the lighter shade and the remaining third a few tones deeper. This will appear to bring the room more into proportion.

COLOUR KEY

1 Mushroom

2 Peach

3 Rose pink

4 Pale mushroom

HOW TO DO IT

Taping the zig-zag on the wall is the most time-consuming part of this project, but the result makes it all worthwhile.

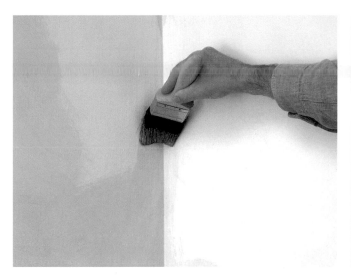

STEP 1 Decide on the height where the zigzag colour meeting point will be, then paint the top half of the wall in the lighter shade to roughly 25mm (1in) below the lower point of the zigzag. Leave this overnight to dry – this is important to prevent the masking tape from lifting the paint as it is removed.

STEP 2 Measure the height to where the top point of the zigzag will be and make a mark. Do this along the wall, and draw a soft pencil line to join the marks. Check it with the level.

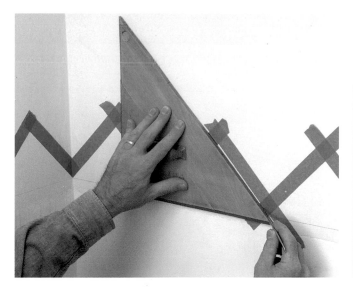

STEP 3 Place a strip of masking tape at a 45° angle from the line to the wall edge. Now place another one at 90° to the first. This is the shape and size of the zigzag pattern. Each following piece is placed at 90° to the previous one and trimmed to give a neat point.

STEP 4 Paint the lower section of the wall using a small roller or paintbrush to paint over the edge of the masking tape. When the paint is almost dry, lift the masking tape carefully, breaking off and disposing of manageable sections as you go along. This way you are less likely to become entangled in a web of painted tape! Use the paintbrush to touch up any pencil guidelines that remain on the lighter shade.

PROJECT
Chair liming and re-covering

YOU WILL NEED:

A wooden (oak or pitch pine) dining chair in need of rescue

A piece of suede large enough to cover the seat or a suede garment to cut up and re-cover the seat

Wire brush

Liming wax

Furniture wax

Fine wire wool

Soft polishing cloth

Scissors

Staple gun

COLOUR KEY
1 Light grey
2 Apricot
3 Silver grey
4 Terracotta

It is always worth looking out for a chair with potential for a make-over. The ideal chair for this project would be oak or pitch pine with a drop-in seat pad. Oak is a beautiful hardwood, whose characteristic grain was often disguised with dark stains and heavy varnish. Strip off all the old coatings to reveal the natural wood beneath. The liming is done with a liming wax, and the chair seat is given a new look with a covering of soft suede – either imitation, or real suede from a leather dealer. An alternative is to use recycled suede from a skirt bought from a charity shop or flea market.

HOW TO DO IT

Bring out the true beauty of oak with this simple liming treatment, then add a new seat cover and transform an old dining chair into a contemporary piece of furniture.

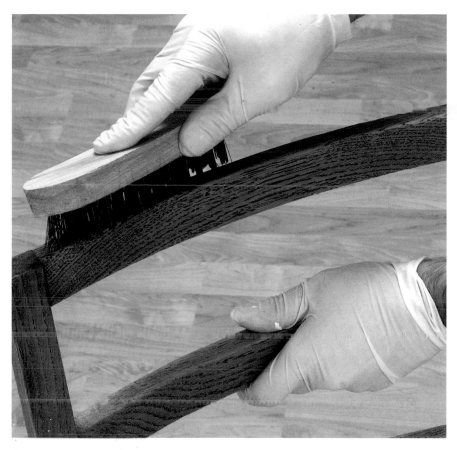

STEP 2 Dip the wire wool into the liming wax and rub the wax into the wood, both with and against the grain.

STEP 1 Save yourself the pain and have the chair professionally dipped in a paint-stripping tank. When it has dried out, check all the joints and re-glue where necessary. Push a wire brush along the surface following the direction of the grain. This is called raking out, and it will get rid of any soft wood or dust trapped in the grooves.

STEP 3 Leave it to dry for about half an hour, then dip a fresh piece of wire wool in furniture polish and rub it over the surface to lift off the liming wax. The grain will show up white where the lime has remained in the grooves. Buff the surface with a soft cloth.

STEP 4 Trim away any thick seams, zips and buttons from the garment, leaving any attractive seaming, which can be used as part of a deliberate design on the seat.

STEP 5 Lay the seat base on the suede and use one staple in the middle of each side to attach the suede to the seat frame.

STEP 6 Staple the suede all the way around the seat frame, pulling it taut and trimming away any excess. Fit the seat back into the chair frame.

3-D effects with colour

Colour can make a wall shimmer, fade, dazzle or confuse. The most obvious 3-D effect is produced by using a light/dark contrast to create a drop shadow. This can create illusions such as simple raised panels, recessed niches or intricate plaster mouldings. Coloured shapes can be shaded to give them form and the shape of a room can be dramatically changed by the introduction of a false sense of perspective. Once you understand the advancing and receding qualities of different colours you can produce very convincing effects.

The Ndbele tribeswomen in South Africa paint their simple mud huts externally with architectural features such as columns, pediments, archways and castellated walls. The background is whitewash, with black outlines and patterns filled in with brilliant colours. It is an idea that can be seen in many parts of the world where paint is used in bold and creative ways to imitate ornate architecture. In Mexico, houses are painted vivid colours with striped bands of contrasting colours. Wall paintings often create 3-D effects and murals are an important part of the local culture.

Trompe l'œil

Expert trompe l'œil painters create convincing illusions such as
• walls of shelves stacked with books
• doorways where they don't exist
• windows looking out on panoramic views and many other special effects.

There is no need to be that ambitious, but there is fun to be had by using 3-D effects to add life and interest to a featureless room.

A painted frieze of light and dark geometric shapes can be drawn out with

templates, and if the angles and the direction of the light are plotted correctly the effect will be simply stunning.

The first of the 3-D projects included in this section shows you how to paint blocks of colour with dropped shadows. This is a very basic 3-D effect that can be used in a striking way or in a very toned-down way, depending on which room in the house you choose to use it.

It can be a popular choice in living rooms, but it may be best to use small blocks of subtle colours – large blocks of primary colours may prove difficult to live with.

The second project offers a major colour contrast that is only slightly toned down with the use of the feathering paint technique to soften the edges of the blocks.

This, too, is an effect that is very easy to achieve but has a stunning result. Because the colours contrast so vibrantly, the blocks will seem to float.

The third project is ideal for use as a wall frieze or door surround and involves painting three diamond shapes to produce a convincing cube effect.

Go on, dive into the world of 3-D!

PROJECT
Blocks of colour with dropped shadow

YOU WILL NEED:

Long rule with a spirit level

Pencil or chalk

Plumb line

Set square

Decorator's masking tape

Colour for blocks

Shadow colour

Small roller and tray

Paintbrush (25mm/1in)

This is the simplest three-dimensional effect, whose impact increases with the size of the shapes. The colours chosen for the blocks can be as subtle or bold as you choose. If the room style is based around neutral colours, then using two tones of stone grey will create a subtle panelled effect. On the other hand, primary colours with black shadows on a white background will make the blocks of colour appear to leap off the wall. Much depends upon the room's shape, size and purpose. But beware – a bedazzling optical effect would soon become tiresome in an everyday living room.

COLOUR KEY

1 Avocado

2 Red salmon

3 Pure blue

4 Black

HOW TO DO IT

Treat your wall as a blank canvas and create this dramatic effect in the boldest of colours. A 45° set square and a ruler with a straight edge are the essential tools for the job.

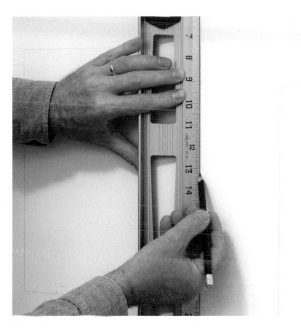

STEP 1 Measure the area and calculate the size and positions of the colour blocks. Drop the plumb line to use as a vertical guide and use the long rule to mark out rectangular shapes in pencil.

STEP 2 Place a strip of masking tape around each of the shapes then apply the colour with the small roller. Leave to dry, then peel off the tape. Leave overnight until bone dry.

STEP 3 Use the set square to draw a shadow box at 45° on one side and the base of each block. Place a strip of masking tape around the shadow area, including the two inside edges of the colour block.

STEP 4 Paint the shadow with the brush and leave the paint to dry before peeling off the tape.

PROJECT
Vibrant contrasts

COLOUR PALETTE

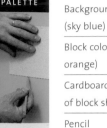

YOU WILL NEED:

Background colour
(sky blue)

Block colour (burnt
orange)

Cardboard template
of block shape

Pencil

Roller and paint tray

Household paintbrush
(75mm/3in)

Softener brush from
paint effects store

This project shows the power of intense colour contrasts, but softens the impact by using a more painterly approach. The paint is applied with a large brush used to feather the edges of the blocks to avoid hard edges.

The orange and blue contrast is sharp and funky. Other vibrant contrasts are yellow and violet, red and green, and lime and purple. Cool colours retreat; warm ones advance.

First paint the wall with the background colour, then draw outlines for the colour blocks using a template. When you fill them with a vibrantly contrasting colour, they will appear to float.

COLOUR KEY
1 Sky blue
2 Burnt orange
3 Vibrant yellow
4 Violet

HOW TO DO IT

A template can be any shape or size. Have fun designing your own or simply follow the pattern used here. This dazzling effect is sure to be a real talking point.

STEP 1 Paint the wall the background colour. Leave to dry.

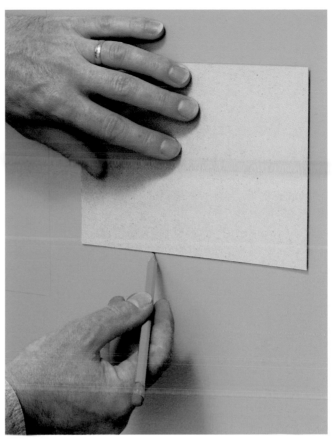

STEP 2 Hold the template against the wall and draw outlines for the colour blocks.

STEP 3 Paint the blocks burnt orange up to the pencil line.

STEP 4 Feather the edges of the blocks before the paint has a chance to dry. Do this by running the softener brush lightly over the paint edge so that it spreads and fades.

PROJECT
Baby block pattern

YOU WILL NEED:

Upholstery foam

3 x photocopies of
the diamond shape

Spraymount

Scalpel

A light colour;
a mid tone and
a dark shadow colour
emulsion or acrylic
paint

3 small foam rollers

3 white dinner plates

Long rule with a
spirit level

Pencil or chalk

This is a traditional patchwork quilt pattern where three diamond shapes are fitted together to resemble a cube. The illusion relies on the top diamond being a mid tone, the left side being light and the right side a darkened tone. It creates a most effective illusion, and a line of them makes a good wall frieze or a door surround. The pattern is printed on the wall using diamonds of upholstery foam, but could also be stencilled if you prefer that effect. The printing method gives the sort of variety seen in a marble mosaic, as each print is different but the three colours remain the same.

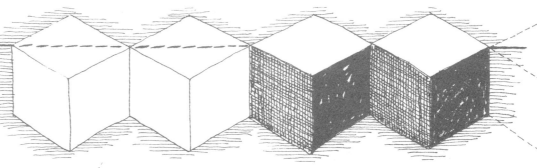

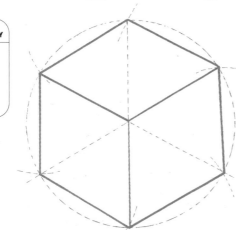

COLOUR KEY

1 Deep orange

2 Grey-blue

3 Orange sorbet

4 Maize yellow

TEMPLATE

The three separate diamond shapes will form a three-dimensional cube, given depth by the use of light, mid and dark tones of colour.

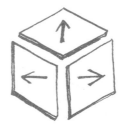

HOW TO DO IT

Buy an off-cut of upholstery foam and try this effect. It is one of the most convincing and easily achieved 3-D patterns, and it is always fascinating to look at.

STEP 1 Apply Spraymount to the photocopies and stick them onto the foam.

STEP 2 Carefully cut out the three diamond shapes. Try to cut each side in one continuous line for a neat edge. The full thickness can be cut through afterwards – it is the printing edge that needs to be straight.

STEP 3 Measure and mark out a top line position for the frieze.

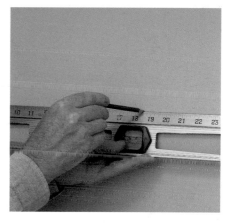

STEP 4 Check with the spirit level that the line is straight.

STEP 5 Put the mid-tone colour on the plate and run the small roller through it. Coat one of the diamond shapes and print the shapes lengthways with the point on the line.

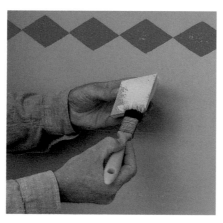

STEP 6 Put the other two colours on plates and use a separate roller for each one. Coat the remaining diamonds with the light and dark tones.

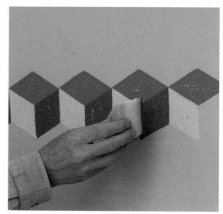

STEP 7 Beginning with the dark colour, print a dark diamond below the mid-tone along its lower right edge. Then print the light tone alongside the dark one. Continue to the end.

COLOUR
PALETTE

Tactile surfaces

We not only need to see a variety of textures, we also need the tactile experience, and we feel soothed, reassured, excited or energised when in touch with different textures. Silk, satin, suede and velvet are warm, sensual and luxurious, whereas cotton, linen and muslin are cool, fresh and practical. There are more textures than there are words to describe them. Some are there for practical and safety reasons, for instance non-slip bathroom flooring. Hard, soft, smooth or rough ,we need a balance of textures in our home.

Man-made fabrics, floorings and furniture are best when they are being themselves rather than a cheap imitation of the real thing. One of the problems with man-made fabrics is that they are of a consistent quality and so lack the characteristic imperfections that make a natural product so attractive.

Seating

Most seating is a combination of hard frame with soft padding, with extra layers of comfort added by cushions, rugs and throws. This is where texture can be used to best effect, either instead of, or as well as adding other colours. A loose-weave mohair throw, a large corduroy bolster, a soft suede cushion or a silk shawl on a sofa will each generate a different layer of comfort. Pashmina shawls are one fashion item that is equally desirable as clothing and soft furnishings, being at home on both shoulders and armchairs. A neatly folded shawl or rug over the arm of a chair looks smart but also offers potential cosiness should you need it. Contemporary style is very much about hard and soft areas, contrasting cool open spaces with soft islands of comfort.

Flooring

Flooring is often the largest area of texture, colour and pattern in a room. Walls and ceilings can be rough, chalky or shiny without physically affecting us, but the floor we walk on has to be comfortable underfoot. There is tremendous choice in flooring, but essentially it needs to be suited to the room's purpose, easy to clean and not too dominating. If you have beautiful wooden boards or polished parquet blocks, then colour and texture can be added with rugs, and after that fitted woven matting is the most homogeneous choice. Rush and coir mats do the same job as wooden floorboards for living rooms, not making too strong a statement yet providing a warm, comfortable, natural and neutral base for most furniture styles and colour schemes. Coloured carpets are the ideal flooring for bedrooms, where bare feet touch the floor. They also have less through traffic and are a good place to use light colours and soft textured carpets which would be impractical elsewhere. The ultimate is cream shagpile carpet, once considered a fashion crime but now back in the style magazines again – and a lot more fun than bare floorboards.

PROJECT
A coloured tissue-paper patchwork wall

YOU WILL NEED:

Tissue paper

Wallpaper paste

Clear matt varnish

A brush to apply it

The colour range for tissue paper is really gorgeous, ranging from hot pinks and purples to soft pastels and all the primaries. Choose a palette of four or five colours and tear random shapes so that none of the paper has a straight-cut edge. The idea is to overlap shapes, building up a collage of colour on an area of wall. The background colour will show through, and should be used to set the overall colour you would like for the wall. Tissue paper is very fine and will tear or wrinkle, but this is part of the effect, so try not to make it look too perfect. The end result will be textured and colourful.

COLOUR KEY

1　Hot pink

2　Deep rose

3　Shaker blue

HOW TO DO IT

Making tissue paper patchwork is not difficult and the transparency gives it a stunning effect reminiscent of stained glass. There are lots of colours to choose from; the pieces can be made smaller or larger if you prefer.

STEP 1 Tear the sheets of paper, reserving enough straight-cut edge pieces to go around the edges of the wall (think of a jigsaw puzzle!).

STEP 2 Paste the wall area to be covered with a thin, even coating of wallpaper paste.

STEP 3 Beginning in the middle of the wall, apply different coloured shapes to overlap each other slightly so that the wall is covered.

STEP 4 When you reach the edges of the wall, use the reserved straight-edged shapes to make a neat edge. When the wall is bone dry, apply a protective coat of matt varnish.

PROJECT
Cane or bamboo wall panels

YOU WILL NEED:

Split cane or bamboo panels to fit the length of a wall

Moulding to finish off edges of the panels to fit the length of the wall

Drill and fine drill bits

Long rule with a spirit level

Stapler gun

Panel pins

Small hammer

One of the hottest new looks around is applied texture, especially using natural material to line interior walls. Cane and bamboo are both ideal materials for this kind of home decoration project. The garden centre is the best place to look for cane or bamboo panelling; it is sold in a range of heights and lengths and is not expensive. Other options for this kind of project include willow and reed panels.

You could fix the panels to wall battens that can be easily removed or, as has been done here, use a staple gun and panel pins to attach the panels to the wall.

COLOUR KEY

1 Earthy orange
2 Chocolate
3 Burnt orange

HOW TO DO IT

Bamboo or cane panels are not expensive but will quite easily transform a room. Before you start this project, paint any areas of the wall that are not going to be covered with bamboo or cane.

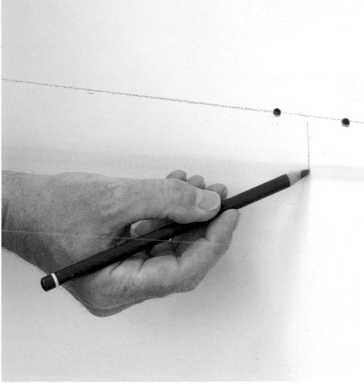

STEP 1 Measure and cut the required lengths of bamboo or cane. Use the fine drill bit to find the positions of the studs in the wall.

STEP 2 Mark the positions on the wall and above the height of the panels so they can be found once the panels are in place.

STEP 3 Smooth the panel up against the wall and use a staple gun or panel pins to fix it to the studs in the wall.

STEP 4 Fix the mouldings along the top and bottom of the panels with panel pins and a small hammer.

PROJECT
Fleece bed surround

YOU WILL NEED:

500mm (20in) fleece, 1.5m (60in) width (depending on bed size), either microfibre or acrylic fleece

Braid

Scissors

Tape measure

PVA adhesive

Fabric adhesive

Pencil

Long rule with spirit level

This project is an extension of the cot bumper, and is intended to create a wall softening transition zone for toddlers when they make the move from sleeping in a cot to a bed pushed up against a wall. Fleece is made in a wide range of bright colours and is very easy to work with because the edges do not fray and will not need to be hemmed. Choose the fabric and braid in a contrasting colour to the wall, or use a deeper shade of the wall colour, perhaps with a contrasting edging braid. Keep the trimming simple if the child is very young because fringe or baubles will not withstand very much tugging!

COLOUR KEY

1 Light turquoise

2 Pure orange

3 Golden yellow

HOW TO DO IT

The fleece is attached to the wall using PVA adhesive. If you prefer not to glue the fabric directly onto the wall, glue the fabric to a sheet of hardboard or 6mm (¼in) plywood first and fix it onto the wall with screws.

STEP 1 Measure the area to be covered and cut the fleece to fit average 1m x 1.5m (3ft x 5ft) – child's bed sizes vary. You need to cover the wall area approximately 500m (20in) up from mattress height. Trim the fleece to the same size.

STEP 2 Draw the shape on the wall in pencil, checking the vertical and horizontal lines with the spirit level.

STEP 3 Spread an even coating of PVA adhesive onto the wall, starting in the middle of the shape and working outwards. Pay special attention to the edges. The PVA dries fast so aim to work quickly.

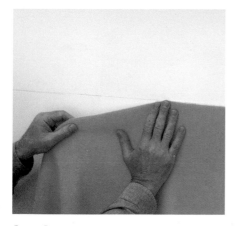

STEP 4 Smooth the fleece onto the PVA with the flat of your hand, keeping pressure light and even so that the fabric does not stretch and distort the shape.

STEP 5 Measure and cut the lengths of braid or trimming ribbon needed for the edging.

STEP 6 Apply fabric adhesive to the back of the braid then run it around the edge of the fleece so that it overlaps slightly onto the wall and completely conceals the raw edge of the fleece.

Colour Highlights

Flashes and splashes of colour in any room will attract the eye and create a more energetic environment. The secret of colour highlighting is that the strongest impact is achieved when the highlight colour is used in moderation. Too much and it becomes a feature, too little and it might be overlooked. In this chapter we take a look at the different elements that go to make up a decorating scheme, and how their colours can be used to add focus to a room. Paintings, plants, rugs, lamps and window treatments are the key areas we focus on.

Introduction

 The idea of a highlight is to attract attention and perhaps at the same time distract the eye from a less deserving area. If colour is to be effective as a highlight, it has to be seen against a neutral or tonally similar background. It will obviously not work in a room that is already a riot of colour. A highlight does not have to be a strongly saturated colour – a flash of pale apricot, for instance, seen against dark grey, would be as effective as a violet purple against baby pink.

CREATING THE EXTRAORDINARY

If the room is mainly used for daytime activities, any colour highlights should be placed within reach of the direct natural light coming from windows, skylights or doors. A room for evening use can be fitted with directional spotlights, as light is imperative to bring any colour to life.

The highlight should stand out and be quite different from the surrounding colour, and its effect should be uplifting.

Choosing colours to use in this way provides an opportunity to follow our colour instincts and introduce our favourite colours. These are often the stronger shades that produce an immediate physical response when we see them, and as this reaction is so subjective it is best to avoid using them over large areas. Many interior designers have built their reputations on their bold use of certain colours in public places or other people's homes, but are revealed to have chosen a neutral palette when their own homes feature in interior design magazines. Large areas of a favourite colour can be too stimulating and exhausting to live with, whereas a small area can be deliciously attractive, bringing the eye back again and again to take pleasure in its beauty.

The right combinations and arrangements of colour are like food for the eyes, and good food makes us feel better. We need to balance what our eyes see in the same way as we do our diets, providing a balance of colours to satisfy our senses without over-indulgence, which leads to the visual equivalent of indigestion.

The colour of the background will help decide which highlights will work best. A strong contrast is important, but this could be one of tone as well as colour. Complementary colours from opposite sides of the colour wheel, such as orange and blue or red and green, create exciting highlights, but must be used in the correct proportions to one another or they will be too competitive. A sage green room, for instance, will be enlivened by a bowl of scarlet dahlias but completely overpowered by a large red rug. Remember that it is with flashes of brilliance that we turn the ordinary into the extraordinary.

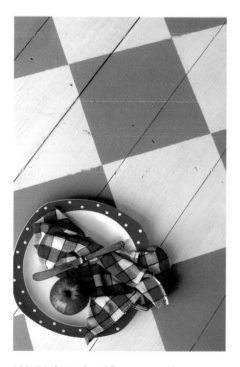

ABOVE **A chequerboard floor can provide a colourful and charming feature.**

LEFT **A simple clear glass vase filled with luscious lilies will inject a sense of grandeur into any room. These are flowers with the look and smell of luxury and opulence. Choose them for their colours – bright pinks, vivid oranges, acid yellows; their shape – waxy curved petals, powdery red stamens and tall firm stems; and for their glamour.**

LEFT **Cushions can be a stylish and effective means of giving a room colour highlights.**

Adding focus

The process of decorating involves a lot of visualisation, preparation, shopping and plain hard work. The inspiration for a colour scheme or room style may have come from something seen in a magazine, on holiday or in someone else's home, but the results are disappointing because, although the general look is the same, something is missing. The room has changed, but with all the hard work completed an extra something is needed to pull the look together. This something is the room's focus.

THE CREATIVE PATH

Most rooms will have some individuality, a feature such as the fireplace, a doorway, a nice floor or perhaps a style of window that becomes the natural focal point. If nothing is striking enough to become an area of focus, then one can be created with colour. This could be done with paint; it could be as simple as painting a contrasting coloured shape on one of the walls, or painting blocks of colour as broad borders for framed pictures. More often, though, it is done by introducing some new element, which could be a painting, a sculptural piece of furniture, a rug or a wonderful plant. This does not necessarily mean spending a lot of money. The art could be a row of pebbles in a straight line; a strangely shaped piece of driftwood displayed on a bright background, or a pile of pine cones sprayed shocking pink. A canvas floorcloth can be painted and stencilled for a fraction of the cost of buying a rug, or you could paint a rug directly onto the floor. It is important to enjoy the decorating process, and taking the creative route is always more rewarding than shopping – well, nearly always!

LEFT **This circular rug has radiating coloured lines that attract the eye to its colour, shape and size. A bare floor is fine for dancing, but rugs make a room much more homely.**

KEEPING THINGS IN PROPORTION

Proportion is very important, as there is a big difference between attracting attention and dominating a room. An exuberant palm in a ceramic pot looks great – as long as it's not so great as to infringe on your space! In just the same way, something that is far too small in proportion to its surroundings doesn't work either. A small handmade designer rug will still attract attention in the middle of a large open expanse of floor, but it will look mean.

SMART BUT SIMPLE

Choosing wisely does not always mean spending a lot of money. One idea which works very well is repetition. Instead of buying one large vase, buy four in the same style but in different colours, and arrange them in a straight line. This will create a colour rhythm and focus, and need not cost very much at all. The same could be done with something completely free, like green-tinged cola bottles, which are design classics. A line of them becomes a sculpture in the right setting.

Fresh flowers are the most reliable way of adding instant focus to a room. Depending on what you choose, flowers can be used to change the mood of the room – they can even be used to reflect your own mood, if you like! For instance, if you're feeling romantic, choose roses; and if you're feeling full of the joys of life and you don't care who knows it, go for lilies. Many flowers come in a whole range of gorgeous colours, so you should have no problem working with your room's colour scheme, and changing the atmosphere throughout the year. An arrangement of striking seedheads from the garden can also make a really stunning display.

If a bunch of flowers seems too much of an indulgence, just buy one or two single stems and angle a spotlight their way. This little trick creates a tremendously cool, contemporary effect.

Window treatments

Windows are one of the main focal points in any room because of the light coming in and the view of the outside world that they reveal. Windows also give us an opportunity to introduce colour and pattern that will flatter the room's colour scheme and pick up on colours used elsewhere in the room. The biggest mistake is to treat the window in isolation without taking the rest of the room into account, because the right window treatment will make any room look a hundred times better.

ABOVE **When a room has a fabulous view, nothing should be allowed to interfere or detract from it. Window frame colours or curtains should create a perfect frame for the view, choosing either a strong contrast as an outline or a harmonious shade to create a more natural progression from room to view. In this room there are no curtains to complicate the scene, and the frames have been painted to match the blue-green of the trees.**

THE RIGHT TREATMENT

There are so many different ways of covering windows, and some solutions will only suit certain situations. Consider whether the room is mainly to be used during the day or at night, what the room's purpose is, and if there are any practical limitations on the type of window treatment that would suit the room. In a room which has direct early morning sunlight, curtains will need black-out linings or blinds; one that is overlooked by other windows will need muslins or nets for privacy, and windows opening onto a busy street will soon make curtains grimy and the chosen fabric will need to be one that will not deteriorate with regular washing.

Sometimes, the view from a window is simply too stunning to conceal – a view of city lights at night, for instance, can be hundred times better than the same view during the day when it would be better obscured by slatted blinds, which would also soften and filter the light. A large picture-window view over a garden or fields will be the room's best feature in daylight, but can make the inhabitants feel too exposed after dark, when thick drapes would make the room feel more intimate. Ruling out specific window treatments is helpful as this will help to narrow down the options and allow you to focus on what will look best.

When in doubt, do something creative and temporary while you decide. If there is a curtain rail, use cotton sheets or saris, draped or with curtain clips.

SUBTLE CO-ORDINATION

The over-co-ordinated decorating style where the same fabric is used for furnishings and curtains is very dated, and looks as impersonal as a hotel or a furniture showroom. Try picking up a theme instead with, for instance, sari-style fabric used for curtains and embroidered silk cushions in matching colours, making a link between the furniture and the window treatment. A crochet white lace panel pinned across a window in a simple Mediterranean-style bedroom will echo the lace cloth on a bedside table. A bright orange roller blind will warm up a shaded north-facing window, and something as simple as a bowl of oranges will match the colour and balance its brilliance in the room.

ABOVE **Simple roller blinds are one of the most economical window treatments and they have the added benefit of obscuring only a small part of the window surface. This means they can be adjusted to allow maximum light into a room when needed or pulled down to reveal the pattern and provide privacy in the evening.**

LEFT **It would be a pity to hide a deep window recess like the one in this cottage. The wooden panelling adds to the sense of perspective and creates the perfect frame for the flower arrangement. Painting a deep recess in light gloss paint will bring more light into the room.**

Window treatments

CURTAINS AND BLINDS

If walls are painted in plain colours then curtains can be patterned in harmonious or contrasting colours, but when using pattern proportion is very important. As a rule, large patterns need large areas and small patterns work best when they are seen at close range.

Coloured transparent fabrics look pale with daylight shining through them, but their colour looks stronger in the evening, especially if the windows are fitted with roller blinds. Blinds are a good way of adding colour to a room, and a contemporary-styled room with a row of windows looks good with a different colour blind in each one. A blind fitted into the window recess can remain in place if curtains are added, but will also look good on its own.

Roman blinds are very easy to make – they hang in folds, and can be made in most fabric weights from heavy canvas to soft voile. They are also the most

economical treatment as they hang as a flat panel to match the dimensions of the window.

When in doubt, choose a plain neutral colour and a classic window treatment rather than something wildly fashionable if you are buying a good quality fabric, as this will not date. If you are on a tight budget, investigate alternative fabrics, especially from street markets near garment-making districts, eg, unbleached calico, bed sheeting, felt, fleece or suit linings.

LEFT **This light, harmonious and thoroughly grown-up living room has been designed around a single shade of lilac. The furniture, woodwork and soft furnishings all match, and the gingham and plaid check of the curtains prevents the effect from becoming too bland.**

ABOVE **Full-length yellow curtains frame this window, and the sun filters through to cast a warm glow of light into the room. The soft furnishing colours used here are cool, with greens and blues mellowed by the brilliance of the yellow curtains. When drawn, the curtains almost fill the wall, making an even bolder yellow statement.**

LEFT **Floral Roman blinds with a dark border are teamed with simple sprigged muslin curtains for these glazed doors. This is a perfect solution for doors that are often in use, as they can be left open to admit the light or closed to provide shade.**

Soft furnishings

 Soft furnishings are the fabrics we use in the home to add character and instil our own personalities. As very few of us undertake the making or even re-upholstery of sofas, armchairs or beds, it's the cushions, shawls, throws, lampshades, tablecloths and bedspreads we add that change something mass-produced into something uniquely ours. The idea is make the room look more attractive and increase the level of comfort, so choose soft fillings and fabrics that are tactile as well as beautiful.

ABOVE **Choose cushions of the same style in different colours to give a harmonious look. These embroidered cushions in purple and olive are exotic and inviting against deep rose chenille upholstery.**

RING THE CHANGES

Soft furnishings can be changed with the seasons, creating a light, airy style in summer and a warm comfort zone for the winter. A sofa can be covered with a fleece throw for winter and cotton for summer. In the days before central heating, this was a normal part of home life, with soft flannel sheets and woolly rugs for winter and crisp cotton sheets and light woven floor mats in summer. Winter curtains were heavy and thick to block out the cold draughts, but summer was a time for net, lace and cheerful cotton prints. Nostalgia can be fun and there is always room for retro style in fashion.

Colour has a huge role to play in soft furnishings, especially if the room is simply decorated in plain colours. A room could be painted off-white with unbleached muslin curtains and chair covers, but still be perceived as colourful if the sofa and chairs were piled with an assortment of vividly coloured cushions, the floor boasted a bright patterned dhurrie and the table lamps had equally vibrant shades. To see how soft furnishings can alter a room's character, first imagine a golden yellow bedroom with an iron bed draped with a rich red velvet bedspread and bolster cushions, then change the bedding to a blue and white striped duvet cover. The whole mood has swung from luxurious and exotic to fresh and breezy. Put the idea into practice by using different fabrics and accessories in your bedroom to spice it up or cool it down to suit the mood.

COLOUR CO-ORDINATION

A monochrome colour scheme can look bland without the right type of soft furnishings. One solution is to choose a range of patterned fabrics that are not usually seen together, in a single colour. This could mean mixing classic patterns such as toile de jouy, stripes, tie-dye circles and floral damask to make a set of unmatched cushions. Keep the rest of the room neutral and leave the cushions to make the colour statement. The beauty of this style of colour co-ordinating is that you can usually buy remnants of expensive fabric in amounts sufficient for cushion covers at a fraction of the cost of buying it off the roll. Make it a rule always to have a rummage in remnant bins anyway, and build up a treasure chest of fabric for future soft furnishing projects.

LEFT **Rich, varied textures and weights of fabrics in shades of yellow.**

ABOVE **The success of creating a Japanese look means taking a no-frills, minimalist approach to both colour and design. Cream, red and black are all the colours you need.**

LEFT **A thick gold and red curtain softens the hard edges of the doorway, and the same colours are picked up in the soft covers of the dining chairs in the background. A band of contrasting colour could be used to join short remnants of superior quality fabrics and create a luxurious draped curtain like this one at a bargain price.**

Painted floors

The idea of painting floors is a very old one that has become popular once again. One of the most attractive aspects of floor painting is how inexpensive it is in comparison to other floor treatments. A floor often needs only a light sanding to prepare it and many paint companies have added special floor paints to their product ranges. If you use conventional paint, add a couple of coats of strong polyurethane varnish to keep the colour fresh or, for a more lived-in style, just let the wear and tear show through.

PREPARING THE FLOOR

If you are thinking of painting the floor and have first to dispose of carpets or old vinyl, it is wise to have a peep underneath to assess the condition of the floorboards. If the flooring has been stuck to the boards with carpet tape you will need to use a sander to remove the sticky tape. If the floor would benefit from a good sanding then it would be best to hire a machine for a day. The sanding machine hire is not hugely expensive but cost of the special sandpaper can add up, so do make it clear in the rental shop that you are sanding to prepare for painting rather than to expose the true beauty of the natural wood. Using a sanding machine does not require great effort but it creates a lot of noise and dust and you have first to remove everything from its path. Once the floor has been sanded it can be wiped over with sugar soap and left to dry before painting.

The most important thing to remember when painting a floor is to begin in the far corner and end in the doorway! A standard paint roller and tray do the job very well unless you are painting the boards different colours, when it is advisable to use a small foam roller or a paintbrush. The paint is best applied in thin coats with adequate drying time between.

Patterned floors can either be stencilled or marked out in chalk and filled in with a paintbrush. One of the most timeless painted patterns is a simple chequerboard which can be painted directly onto floorboards or onto

sheets of hardboard tacked over the boards if you prefer a smoother 'marble' finish.

There are several ways of painting a chequerboard, which can be done diagonally or horizontally. Masking tape can be used to outline the squares. It makes painting easier, but mask and paint only a few squares at a time because it can cause confusion and ruin the pattern over a large area. The simplest method is to mark out the floor in pencil or chalk by drawing round a square template. The stark contrast of black and white can be very unforgiving of any wobbly edges, so choose grey, coffee brown or sage green and off-white instead for a softer but very stylish flooring effect.

SPECIAL FLOOR PAINTS

You can now buy paint made specially for vinyl floors, which means an end to the days of putting up with nasty patterns when you move into a new place, just because the flooring is in too good a condition to justify replacing it. All you need is a pot of paint and a roller to transform a bad floor with a tasteful matt dusky blue, sandy yellow or barn red. Now that's progress!

There are also specialist paints for concrete floors that give a more finished, homely look. Concrete is a cold indoor flooring material suitable only for warm climates or conservatories. It is popular in the South of France, where stunning patterned floors are created with inlays of beach pebbles.

Painting a floor

YOU WILL NEED:

Primer for bare wood
or undercoat

One colour of floor
paint (or use
emulsion paint
with heavy-duty
polyurethane varnish)

A 50mm (2in)
household paintbrush

A large roller and tray
for the primer and
varnish if using

Clear heavy-duty
matt or gloss varnish

Masking tape

Once you have decided to paint a floor, everything will have to be removed from the floor area. Examine the floorboards closely, checking for any protruding nails, which should be banged in using a hammer with a nail punch. Splintered boards must be sanded and any holes filled with a good quality wood filler. Sand the floor lightly, then sweep up all the dust and wash the boards with a sugar soap solution to get rid of any grease. A proper floor paint will give the best finish and last the longest; otherwise, apply two coats of floor quality varnish after the paint.

HOW TO DO IT

Painting a floor in a single colour could not be simpler. It does not take long and the effect will be one of instant freshness.

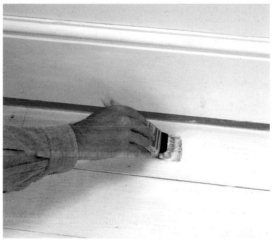

STEP 1 Mask off the skirting boards to floor level.

STEP 2 Begin with the brush, painting the primer into the edges of the floor, right into the corners and up to the masking tape.

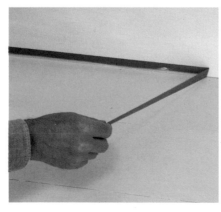

STEP 3 Then apply the primer to the rest of the boards with the roller, beginning in the far corner and painting along the length of the floorboards. Leave to dry.

STEP 4 Apply the floor paint in exactly the same way. It should not be applied too thickly, and two thin coats will always give a better finish than one thick one.

PAINTED FLOORS: PROJECT TWO
Stripes of pastel colours

YOU WILL NEED:

Primer for bare wood
or undercoat

Three colours of
floor paint (or use
emulsion paints
with heavy-duty
polyurethane varnish)
pastel pink, lilac
and powder blue are
used here

Small roller trays (x 3)

Small foam rollers
(x 3) or a 50mm (2in)
household paintbrush

A large roller and tray
for the primer and
varnish if using

Clear heavy-duty matt
or gloss varnish

Masking tape

Floorboards are arranged in a striped pattern, which makes it very easy to pick them out in different colours and make a special feature floor. The floor is prepared in the usual way with a good washing, sanding, filling and priming. The colours should be chosen to suit the room's purpose and need not be strong or even obvious contrasts. A child's playroom can be painted in bright primaries or the seaside pastels, for example. A very gradual tonal colour change will produce the effect of fading or shading, or you could introduce a pattern with the colours reversed.

HOW TO DO IT

A transparent colour like a woodwash is applied directly onto the wood without a primer or undercoat. This will allow the grain to show through.

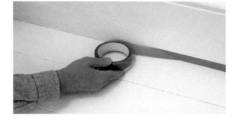

STEP 1 Run masking tape around the skirting board at floor level, then apply a coat of primer or undercoat and leave it to dry.

STEP 2 Begin by applying the pastel pink to the floorboard furthest from the door. Paint each third board in this colour and leave them to dry.

STEP 3 Paint the lilac next, carefully cutting in along the painted board edge. Paint all the lilac boards then leave them to dry.

STEP 4 Paint the blue boards last, cutting in carefully along both edges. Leave the floor to dry overnight.

STEP 5 Apply one or two coats of clear matt or gloss varnish. Take care not to apply the varnish too thickly. Two thin coats are stronger than one thick one.

STEP 6 Finally, peel off the masking tape around the skirting board edges and stand back to admire your masterpiece.

Painting a chequerboard floor

YOU WILL NEED:

Floor paint or woodwash in two colours

Primer or undercoat

Thick cardboard for a template (30cm x 30cm/12in x 12in)

Stanley or other craft knife to cut out the template

Carpenter's pencil or a chalk pencil

Masking tape

A 50mm (2in) broad household brush

A 12mm (½in) square tipped brush or artists' brush for edges

There are several different approaches for painting a chequerboard floor. If the room is a regular rectangle it is important to centre the pattern, dividing the room into quarters and beginning the pattern with a block of four squares in the centre of the room. If you are painting an irregular hallway or a small room it is not as important. The design can be arranged as a horizontal grid or on the diagonal – here it is horizontal, making use of the shape and grain of the floorboards. Painting the skirting boards and any other woodwork in one of the floor colours will give an integrated look.

HOW TO DO IT
The effect is charming and must look deliberately painted, so don't be tempted to fill gaps between old floorboards.

STEP 1 Draw a square onto a piece of stiff cardboard (the width of two floorboards for a large square or one for a small pattern) and cut it out with a strong craft knife.

STEP 2 If you are using a primer or undercoat, apply this to the floor first. Leave it to dry.

STEP 3 Apply the lightest colour to the whole floor surface next and leave it to dry.

STEP 4 Find the centrepoint of the room by running two pieces of string between the opposite corners. Draw the shapes at the intersection, using the template and a pencil.

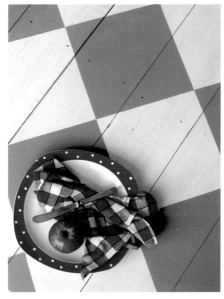

STEP 5 Paint the edges of the square first using the small square-tipped brush.

STEP 6 Use the broader brush to fill in the square and continue in the same way. If you are using a protective varnish, apply with a large foam roller when the squares are dry.

Picture gallery

 The pictures you choose to put on the wall can say more about who you are and what you like than almost anything else in the room. The idea may sound intimidating, but it is far more important to surround yourself with images and colours that give you pleasure than to woo any would-be art critics. Don't restrict your displays to the conventional paintings, prints and photographs – be adventurous and let your creativity flow freely.

FUN ON THE WALL

Hang up anything you like – this could be clothing, hats, games boards, plates, travel tickets, tea packets, circus posters or old property deeds. Try photocopying and scanning – it's a great way to obtain arty images for the walls. Big enlargements of small copperplate signatures and seals make superb graphic images, and small sections of photographs of landscape or flowers can be blown up to make abstract colour compositions.

Original art does not have to cost a fortune, and it is well worth patronising art college shows and local galleries.

Black-and-white photographs are often more dramatic than colour. Use fine black frames to show them off.

BELOW **This colourful corridor contains many small pictures. The pictures are mostly photographs hung at eye level and above it, which is practical when space is limited and the subject matter demands close examination.**

PICTURE-HANGING TIPS

✳ If you are only hanging one picture on a wall, it will either need to be large enough to make a statement that fills a wall on its own or to be hung off-centre, otherwise it will look out of proportion.

✳ Never hang a large, heavy picture above a small one.

✳ When hanging a single row of odd-sized pictures along a wall, fix them so that an imaginary horizontal centre-line runs through them all. The heights will vary but the eye level remains constant.

✳ Make even more of a favourite picture by surrounding the frame with a painted coloured border on the wall.

✳ Framed pictures need to create a balanced effect on the wall, so perhaps one medium-sized picture in one half of the wall is set against a group of three small pictures on the other side.

✳ A wall filled with pictures needs to have a mixture of small and large set out in a pleasing way as well, so that the frames are not too weighty in any one area.

LEFT Arranging art on a wall can be an art in itself. This room has pale neutral walls with an interesting arrangement of pictures in a wide variety of styles, colours and media. A perfect sense of balance has been created.

※ Don't hang pictures too high up the wall, or too low down – keep them around eye level.

※ When you group pictures together, try to see them as colours and tones rather than subject matter. If you half-close your eyes this will help to block the detail and reveal the 'bigger picture'.

※ Lay a group of pictures to be displayed together out on the floor first before putting any fixings in the wall so that you can plot the shape and spaces of the whole arrangement.

※ Begin by examining the walls, checking for pipework and electric cables. There will be water pipes near the radiators, and electric cables run horizontally or vertically near any plugs and switches.

※ Different walls need different fixings, and you need to tap the wall to discover whether it is a cavity wall or plastered brickwork.

※ On a cavity wall you will need to use screws with fixings that grip the back of the wall panel as the screws are tightened. If using a hook, fit it onto the screw before you tighten it, as the backing will drop down into the wall cavity when you remove the screw.

※ A solid wall is suitable for single or multiple brass hooks fitted with masonry nails, which enter the wall at an angle. The shallow three-prong plastic hooks work by spreading the weight, but are only effective if the plaster is in good condition.

※ Heavy pictures are best hung from bolts fitted into drilled and plugged holes.

※ Picture-hanging hooks come in a range of shapes and sizes, and it is important to make sure that the fixings you use are strong enough to support the weight of the picture.

※ Fit D-rings or screw eyes to the back of the picture and thread with taut picture wire. It is vital that these are perfectly aligned for the picture to hang level.

※ Position the picture on the wall and make a mark at the top centre. Measure the distance from the taut wire to the top of the frame and make a mark below the first one. This is the wall fixing position.

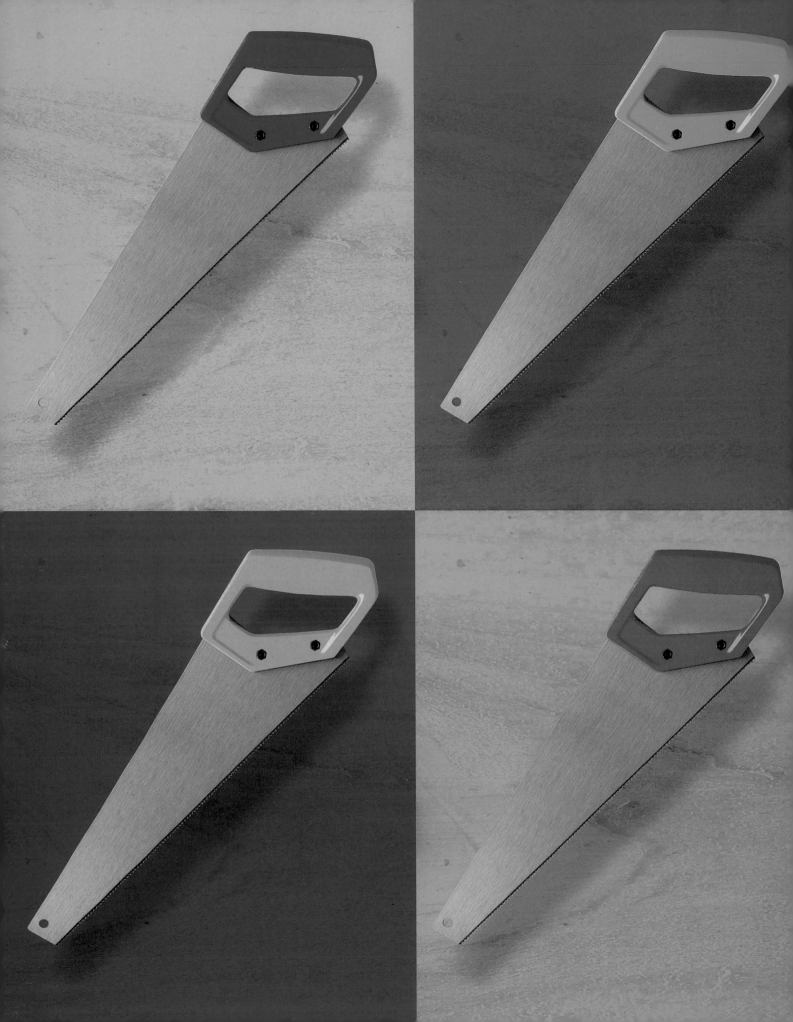

Creating a Style with Colour

The rich variety of historical and cultural influences in our world, as well as the differences between urban or rural environments and hot or cool climates, have ensured that certain colour combinations have become synonymous with particular places. Regional traditions often begin when people use materials available locally, such as lime for whitewash or earth pigments for colouring. A familiar local style is established, which people follow even after other choices have become available.

Introduction

Colours can evoke such strong memories and associations that they transport us to faraway places. In this chapter there are projects designed to help you create a sense of place. Whether you prefer the faded earthy colours of walls in the back streets of Venice to the gilded grandeur of its hotels along the Grand Canal, or the perfumed lavender hills of Provence to the palm trees, striped awnings and pink umbrellas of Cannes, getting the colours right is the vital first step towards recreating the style.

ABOVE **The spirit of Provence conjured up with colour and pattern. The green of the wall has been created by layering three different colours: yellow, blue-green and yellow-green.**

ABOVE **Indian colours defy all the rules and succeed every time. The key to decorating in this style is to use highly saturated colour at its full intensity. If it looks too bright in the tin, then it's perfect!**

COUNTRY STYLES

The chapter begins with a focus on country style, beginning with the most urban, modern take on the country theme, in which the emphasis is on muted, soft background colours and natural fabrics.

The country theme is carried on into New England, with a Shaker peg rail and a set of star sconces. Shaker-style features peg rails around the walls of every room, and no American country home would be complete without some reference to the flag. Then we include an English country look, a combination of new and old country-house style. The colours are bright and modern but the country garden atmosphere remains the same.

STYLES FROM AROUND THE WORLD

Scandinavia is a collective name for the countries around the Baltic Sea and the Arctic Ocean. The colours used here often reflect the sky and the landscape – white, grey blue and yellow. There is a tradition of bold wall painting, and the roller stripe pattern could be made more ornate with hand-painted spots or flowers.

Moroccan colours and style are used for the Moorish Casbah projects, with an arched bedhead painted onto a wall and, because tiling is so much a part of Moroccan style, there is a simple mosaic mirror frame project.

The Indian room is brilliantly coloured, inspired by bright sari fabrics with a touch of pure gold in the stamped detail and border pattern.

LEFT **Most Moorish colours are made using natural earth pigments and the most typical shades are pink, orange, terracotta and blue-green. The deep intense blue, which echoes the night sky of the desert, is the one colour we most associate with this style and is worth seeking out from a specialist paint company. Assemble a mixture of Moroccan textiles and pierced tin lanterns for the full Casbah effect.**

ROMANY AND RUSTIC STYLES

Next up is Romany, which mixes Eastern European folk art and bargeware style. The folk patterns of all travelling people have a lot in common, and the two window projects included here show how to give your kitchen window the Romany treatment.

The rustic farmhouse colours of Tuscany are based on earth pigments and reflect the colours of the fields. The rich red brown, yellow ochre and pale faded viridian green are typically Tuscan. There is an easy woodwork project here, showing how to make a key cupboard for the hallway that looks like a small shuttered window set into a rustic wall. The heat of Provence is offset by the brilliant blue Mediterranean Sea and the colours here are bright and lively. The pattern on the chair is traced and hand-painted in the traditional way. Tablecloths are a key feature of the Provençal kitchen style and, trimmed with simple yellow rick-rack braid, this one is very easy to make.

ECO, URBAN AND BESIDE THE OCEAN

The next projects have more to do with a style than a particular place. The Natural Palette is inspired by eco style. Soft, muddy colours, chalky finishes and natural materials are combined in a cool, calm and contemporary way.

The Urban Minimalist combines few possessions with perfect taste and a limited colour palette. Here the colour lilac is chosen for its calming effect and the floating shelf allows nothing to interfere with its horizontal line. Industrial Modern is a take on loft living style, where a home is made inside an industrial space. Here steel flooring, pulleys and exposed metal girders are the state of the art. The projects show how to give your floor an unusual make-over and how to make a shelving unit supported by breeze blocks.

Beside the Ocean shows how to give your dining area a beach hut holiday feeling with shiny white wood panelling surrounded by plenty of fresh bright colours. And if your idea of a holiday is more Ocean Drive than bucket and spade, the final Miami Pastel projects could be just what you're looking for.

We are all unique individuals with our own colour preferences and passions. The projects in this chapter reach out in so many directions and cover a wide range of decorating ideas, skills and challenges. Be inspired and take this opportunity to nail your own favourite colours to the mast.

COLOUR
PALETTE

Modern country

Country style is about blending in with your surroundings, bringing the outdoors inside and creating a comfortable, harmonious living space. Traditionally this took place on a farm or around the edge of the town where suburbs and fields merge, but now urban country style proclaims everyone's right to a piece of the country – even those with high-rise city homes. Modern country is about choosing the right colours from a limited traditional palette and combining them with weathered textures and homespun accessories.

Colours like buttermilk, moss green, rust red and blue grey all promote a calm atmosphere. Plaster pink, soft golden yellow and terracotta add warmth, and dark green and brown are good deep natural colours.

This is not a cluttered look, although a few genuine country pieces like a birdhouse, stoneware pottery or a weathervane will give an air of country authenticity. The trick is to celebrate simplicity and craftsmanship without resorting to the coolness of minimalism.

Strip and wax the floorboards if they are worth exposing, or paint them if not. In a large room where the floor is less than perfect, you could try a painted chequer-board floor. They are quite easy to do and look great in soft colours like pale green or grey and white.

Keep it natural

Walls are painted in pale country colours to make the most of the room's natural light. Patterns can be introduced with simple graphic stencils, but avoid anything fussy or overtly pretty. Keep the colour scheme natural and save the strong colours for accents, rather than making a feature of them.

Perfect accessories

Modern country patterns are stripes, checks and plaids and the key motifs are letters, numerals, stars and simplified natural shapes like fruit, vegetables, animals and flowers.

Textures include basketweave, wrought iron, linen and genuinely distressed old pieces of furniture or vintage textiles. The combination of good modern design and carefully selected flea market finds are what give this style its charm. Look out for wooden kitchen chairs – a mixture of different styles can be co-ordinated by painting them using the same shade or several harmonious colours.

If your windows frames are new and far from country in style, then drape the real windows with fine muslin. Look out for an old wooden window frame in a salvage yard which can be fitted with a mirror and hung on the wall as a fake window feature – the effect is surprisingly good, especially if you choose what is reflected with care. Don't be afraid to use good modern design with this look – old and new are fine together, just combine good country colours, natural materials and interesting one-off objects for an individual modern country style.

MODERN COUNTRY: PROJECT ONE
Painting a five-board bench

YOU WILL NEED:

A bench – or 5 boards to construct your own

Rust red/orange paint in any matt finish

Turquoise matt paint

Gloss varnish

White candle

Medium grade sandpaper

Wire wool

Paintbrush (50mm/2in)

Background colours:
Buttermilk cream for walls, Natural board or matting floor, Olive green woodwork

The bench used here has been constructed to a traditional pattern using rough timber, to create an instant country antique. These benches have been made all over the world in many shapes and sizes – essentially they have a nice smooth plank top, two ends cut into legs at the base, and two side pieces.

It is a simple design that endures because it is easy and it works well.

These days they are displayed as country antiques, but once every home would have had a small five-board bench that would double-up as a seat for a small child and a single step for reaching high shelves.

COLOUR PALETTE

1

2

3

4

5

COLOUR KEY

1 Sea green

2 Bluebell

3 Powder blue

4 Khaki brown

5 Duck egg blue

HOW TO DO IT
Use colours with a good contrast in order to make the most of this fun painting technique.

STEP 1 Apply one coat of the rust red paint. This thick covering coat must be bone dry before the next stage.

STEP 2 Rub the candlewax on all the edges of the top plank, plus lightly across two 'sitting' areas on the surface. Also rub along the edges of the legs and the side planks. The candlewax will resist the next coat of paint, although this will not be obvious at first.

STEP 3 Apply a single coat of the bright turquoise paint, and leave the bench to dry.

STEP 4 Using the wire wool, rub away the paint in all the areas where you rubbed the candlewax. After initial resistance it should come off quite easily. Now use the sandpaper to rub away some of the red below to reveal some of the wood. Don't rush this job – the aim is to replicate the effect of many years of family life, so it is worth taking a little time over it!

STEP 5 Apply two or three coats of gloss varnish to the turquoise parts, leaving the rubbed areas matt. This will enhance the illusion of layers applied over the years.

MODERN COUNTRY: PROJECT TWO
Muslin no-sew curtains

COLOUR PALETTE

YOU WILL NEED:

Iron

Ironing board

Scissors

Tape measure

Straight edge

25mm (1in) width bonding tape

Curtain width muslin (1.5m/5ft preferable)

500mm (20in) of same width grey linen or fine cotton lawn

Curtain pole

Pole supports

COLOUR KEY

1 Ivory
2 Ice blue
3 Faded cornflower
4 Soft purple

Butter muslin is soft and not too transparent. It filters the light and obscures the view both into and out of a room. The unbleached cream fabric has just enough weave to be interesting, and lets in just enough light to show this off. The muslin is a very lightweight fabric and as such is ideal to use with bonding tape and an iron. The curtains are hung from a pole threaded through a fold-over casing at the top and finished with a binding hem of dove-grey linen which adds just the right amount of weight to ensure that the curtains hang really well.

HOW TO DO IT

No-sew muslin curtains can be made very quickly and the finish is often neater than stitching. Take time to measure and turn the hems evenly and avoid touching the bonding tape with the iron.

STEP 1 Measure the window. The curtains should not be too full, so allow the width plus half again to give a slightly gathered look. Measure the length from the pole to the floor and add 100mm (4in) for the fold-over casing. At the bottom the raw edge will be enclosed in the band of linen. Place the curtain lengths on the ironing board and press a folded 20mm (¾in) hem.

STEP 2 Draw a line 80mm (3¼in) from the first fold. Iron the bonding tape on the line. Peel off the backing and fold the top section over. Press to bond the two sides together.

STEP 3 Cut out the grey binding strips and turn over and press a small seam to fold in the raw edges.

STEP 4 Place a strip of bonding tape along each of the folded seams and press with an iron to bond. Now fold them in half lengthways and press along the fold.

STEP 5 Place the raw bottom edges of the muslin inside the folded linen edgings. Pin them in place. Peel off the backing, one side at a time, and iron to bond the fabrics.

STEP 6 Press the curtain lengths and feed them onto the pole.

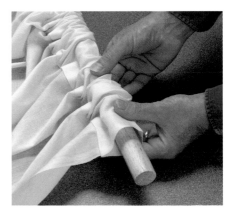

New England

The New England style contains elements of the Maine coast, Shaker, Amish and American Folk Art, and could also be called New Yorker's Retreat style – simplicity as interpreted by the wealthy. The East Coast of America is where the European settlers first landed and cultures merged. There is a mixture of preserved European traditional crafts, local materials and new world aspirations. In the countryside, picket fences surround clapboard houses with rocking chairs on their verandas.

Pay a visit to the library to look at books on the Amish and Shakers, whose quilting and furniture making skills are at the heart of this style. The furniture has a simple elegance and the quilts were constructed within the strict religious boundaries that forbade unnecessary decoration. This pared-down approach to design gives their work a contemporary feel.

The Maine coast style is light and airy, with lots of pale wood, flag and lighthouse references, handhooked rugs, slatted wooden chairs and painted canvas floorcloths. The style is comfortable and casual. There is a real reverence for anything old, from farm stall signs to iron gates or vintage quilts, but this lifestyle relies on just the right mixture of old, new and repro to provide the minimum housework and maximum leisure time.

Mellow warmth

To get the New England country look right, you should use historical American colours in shades reminiscent of those originally derived from earth, mineral and plant pigments – rich, deep rusty red, blue-grey, sky blue, deep green, golden yellow, red-brown, cream and yellow ochre.

Combinations of deep red, black and yellow, or cream and rust red with deep brown woodwork, give a mellow warmth. Keep the main colours slightly muddy and add accents of brilliant colours with tinware, rugs, cushions and pictures.

Seaside style

The seaside style is lighter and brighter, making use of a lot of white to reflect the sun and sea. Faded seaside colours like pale sea green, grey and sky blue combine well with rich bright red and deep navy blue. Driftwood or polished light natural wood looks good, but dark wooden furniture is too heavy for this style. Windows can be shuttered or curtained with plain cotton canvas. If curtains are needed for warmth at night, use blankets with contrasting blanket-stitch edges at the windows. Limit your paint colour palette to a selection of those mentioned, and look out for authentic coastal collectables such as shell pictures, ships in bottles, ropes, anchors etc. But remember to keep it quite bare with a few key objects, and avoid clutter or your airy Maine style will start to resemble a Cornish pub!

NEW ENGLAND: PROJECT ONE
A Shaker-style peg rail

YOU WILL NEED:

50mm x 25mm (2in x 1in) PAR timber, the length of your wall

Wooden pegs or 2m (6ft) of 25mm dowel

25mm (1in) spade bit

Drill

Medium grade sandpaper

Wood glue

Straight edge with a spirit level

Tape measure

Pencil

Wall plugs

No 6 masonry and countersink bit

60mm (2¼in) No6 countersink screws

Wood filler

Primer

Shaker blue paint

Paintbrush

COLOUR KEY

1 Cool light blue
2 Sand brown
3 Pale pistachio
4 Rose pink

The Shakers were a religious group who lived communally. They needed plenty of clear floor space for their meetings, where they performed a peculiar shaking dance, so they hung their chairs from rails on the wall. The Shakers are famous for their simple but beautifully crafted furniture, much of which was 'built in' to keep the rooms plain-looking, although they found ways of adding decorative touches without breaking the religion's strict guidelines on ornament. Shaker style has become very popular in the past decade and fits in very well with the modern trend for de-cluttering.

ALTERNATIVE COLOUR SUGGESTION:
Deep cherry red on a yellow ochre wall

HOW TO DO IT

Peg rails can be positioned at the most useful height for any room – up high in the bathroom or low down in a child's bedroom.

STEP 1 Cut the timber lengths to fit. Mark the positions for the fixings (one screw per metre of rail). Drill out the holes and mark the positions on the wall roughly 1.5m (4ft) from the floor. Drill and plug the holes.

STEP 2 Mark out the positions for the pegs along the rail. They should not be too close together; consider the room's proportions and allow a spacing of 300mm–500mm (12in–20in). Fit the spade bit to the drill and make the holes for the pegs (at an angle of 45°).

STEP 3 If using dowel, cut it into 100mm (4in) lengths for the pegs. Smooth the exposed ends to a neat rounded finish and rub the sides of the 'sinking' ends on the sandpaper to slim them slightly so that they fit snugly into the drilled holes.

STEP 4 Paint the pegs and the rail before you fit them together or attach them to the wall. When the paint has dried, squeeze wood glue into the holes and coat the sinking ends of the pegs. Tap them in position, then wipe away any excess glue. Leave to set.

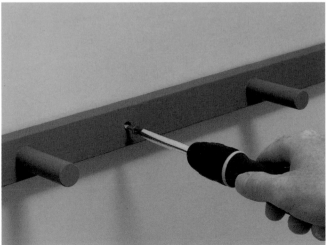

STEP 5 Finally, screw the peg rail onto the wall, then cover the screw-heads with wood filler and touch up with paint once it has dried.

NEW ENGLAND: PROJECT TWO
A painted folk-art star

YOU WILL NEED:

To make one large
star – 250mm x
250mm (10in x 10in)
piece of old pine, plus
small offcut for shelf

Star pattern template

Bench with a clamp

Tenon saw or a jigsaw

Drill with No4 bit

Medium grade
sandpaper

2 x 50mm (2in) No6
screws

Cherry red paint
(acrylic)

Deep-blue paint
(acrylic)

White paint (acrylic)

Beeswax polish and
a brush to apply it

Paintbrushes

A piece of wire and
a nail for hanging up
the star

COLOUR KEY

1 Pure red

2 Almost white

3 Pale sage

4 Deep cornflower

Stars and stripes appear in many forms in American decorating. Genuine folk-art is wonderful, but reproduction objects like this star are fun to make, and help to reinforce the Maine coast theme. Make just one large star or a group of smaller, different-coloured ones. The project shows how to make the most of the grain of an old piece of wood by painting then rubbing back the star and waxing it, or use new pine and give it a similar treatment by applying two different-coloured paints, then rubbing back the top coat in places with sandpaper in places to reveal the colour below. Stark colour contrasts are best for this effect.

TEMPLATE

Draw a pattern based on this star shape. The star made here measured 200mm (8in) from point to point and the small shelf for the candle was 75mm (3in) square.

SUGGESTION

Make a group of small stars in the flag colours and hang them together on the wall as candle sconces (never leave candles in a room unattended as they present a fire risk!).

HOW TO DO IT

A jigsaw makes short work of cutting out these star shapes. Practise your cutting technique on scrap wood before you go onto the real thing.

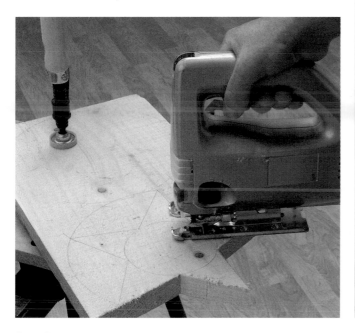

STEP 1 Transfer the pattern onto the wood. Clamp the wood to the bench and, using the tenon saw or jigsaw, carefully cut out the star shape. If you are using a jigsaw then it will be easiest to drill holes at the inner points, insert the blade and cut outwards away from them.

STEP 2 Sandpaper the edges of the star to round them off a bit and to tidy up the inner and outer points. Mark the position for the small shelf and drill two screw holes through the star, then fix it in place from the back using 2 x 50mm (2in) No6 screws.

STEP 3 Apply a coat of red paint and leave to dry.

STEP 4 Rub back the paint around the edges and also rub gently with the grain so that the ridges are revealed. Fix the wire to the back of the star and hang it from a nail, folk style.

COLOUR
PALETTE

English country

The English country cottage is a very cosy and welcoming place where there are roses and honeysuckle around the door in summer and usually a freshly baked cake for tea. In the winter time there will always be a log fire burning in the grate and a soft wool shawl draped over the back of the sofa for that little bit of extra warmth. If you get the look right, visitors should immediately feel so at home that they flop down in a comfortable chair, put their feet up and ask for a cup of tea. In fact, you may have to use force to evict them!

English country style is eclectic, and only really works well when old and new are mixed together. Aim for the impression that furniture and accessories have been passed down through the family for several generations. If you are starting from scratch, shop around at antique markets, boot sales and craft fairs. The right framed mirror or china bowl can make all the difference and need not cost a fortune – imperfections, chips and worn edges actually enhance the look.

Pattern is one of the key ingredients, and many different styles can be successfully combined, including woven woollen plaids, Indian and Turkish rugs, tapestries, plain and floral cotton chintz, damask and lace.

Old and mellow

Floral patterned fabrics are now produced in soft faded colours, or you could search out genuine vintage fabrics at jumble sales or flea markets. One old chintz curtain can make a whole set of plump cushions if you're handy with a sewing machine.

In old country cottages with exposed beams, walls are usually rough plaster painted white, pink or creamy yellow. Low ceilings and small windows can make rooms dark and gloomy, but by painting window recesses glossy white you can virtually double the amount of incoming natural light. Another trick is to position mirrors opposite windows to reflect the light back into the room.

Faking it

If you don't have a sweet little beamed country cottage, but still want to decorate in the English Country style, the first thing to consider is the proportions of the room. Even the most boxy plain room can be made to look a lot cosier with the right wall treatment, colours and lighting. Walls can be tongue and groove panelled up to picture rail height with a shelf running above the panelling. Or apply a rough textured paint to give the impression of an uneven surface and rough plasterwork. Stencilling works well on rough surfaces and is perfect in a country setting. Patterns can either be cut at home, taking inspiration from textiles in the room, or bought ready-cut.

The key colours are taken straight from the cottage garden: soft powder blue, cream, all shades of pink, pale, moss and grass green, brown and brick red.

ENGLISH COUNTRY: PROJECT ONE
A rose-stencilled wall

YOU WILL NEED:

Powder blue paint for background

Sample pots of two pinks

Sample pot of green

Stencil material (mylar or stencil card if you prefer), or buy a ready-cut rose stencil

Spraymount

Scalpel or craft knife

3 stencil brushes

3 white saucers

Plumb line

Square of card (to mark distance between motifs)

If you like pattern and have uneven walls, then stencilling is the way to go, as wallpaper requires walls that are smooth and even. This is a very romantic, feminine style for a pretty bedroom. The blue rose-patterned walls have a look of faded textiles and combine well with lace, muslin and plenty of vintage floral fabrics used for cushions and bed covers. The walls provide a perfect backdrop for traditional bedroom furniture like dressing tables, Lloyd Loom chairs, iron bedsteads and wardrobes. Keep a look-out for pretty old vases, mirrors and lamps that will add authenticity to the look.

COLOUR KEY

1 Soft peacock blue
2 Deep rose pink
3 Pale pistachio
4 Rose pink

TEMPLATE

Copy this pattern or enlarge it using the grid system. We used the rose pattern at the size of 60mm (2½in) across. The stencil can be cut from waxed card or special stencil plastic available from craft stores.

HOW TO DO IT

Stencilling a wall pattern is quicker than putting up wallpaper and also a lot cheaper. Use the smallest amount of paint on your brush and practise on paper before you tackle the wall.

STEP 1 Make the pattern for the stencil. Coat the back of the pattern with Spraymount and stick it onto the stencil material. Use a sharp craft knife and cut out the stencil carefully.

STEP 2 Peel off the paper pattern, then spray the back of the stencil with Spraymount and leave it to become tacky.

STEP 3 Hang the plumb line 250mm (10in) from one corner of the wall and position the card with the line running through two corners. Make a pencil mark at each corner, then move the card down, placing the top point on the lowest mark, and repeat to skirting. Mark up the whole wall in this way.

STEP 4 Position the stencil and smooth it onto the wall. Put the paints on the saucers and dab off brushes with kitchen paper so little remains on the brush.

STEP 5 Begin stencilling with the dark pink in the middle of the rose, then move on to the pale pink for the outer petals. Lift the stencil to check on the result as you go.

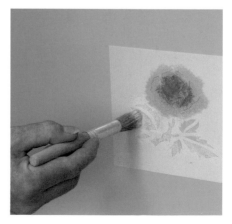

STEP 6 Use the green paint for the leaves and stem. Lift the stencil to check the result. Position it on the next mark and repeat the pattern until the wall is covered with roses.

ENGLISH COUNTRY: PROJECT TWO
A painted chair with a new cushion cover

COLOUR
PALETTE

1

2

3

4

FOR THE CHAIR YOU WILL NEED:

A chair to make over

Medium grade sandpaper

Pale green paint

White matt acrylic primer

Paintbrush

FOR THE CUSHION COVER YOU WILL NEED:

Floral fabric to cover your chair seat

Scissors

Pins

Thread

Sewing machine (or just a stapler if the seat is a drop-in type)

COLOUR KEY

1 Pistachio green
2 Sugar pink
3 Deep leaf green
4 Pale lilac

Start off by going shopping for an old chair in need of some tender, loving care. It should not be difficult to pick up a bargain, as dealers go for matching pairs or sets of four or more. The ideal chair would be wooden with a pretty shape and an upholstered seat. A Lloyd Loom chair is another option, and a frilled loose cushion could be made if a seat is not upholstered. The chair used in this project is a traditional bentwood design with a hard round seat in need of a soft cushion. If your chair has an upholstered seat, cut out a new one using the previous cover as a pattern and staple it neatly in place.

HOW TO DO IT: THE CHAIR

Decide where you are going to put your chair before you buy it, and choose one that will suit the space. It is not necessary to strip all the old paint or varnish from the chair – simply rub it down for painting.

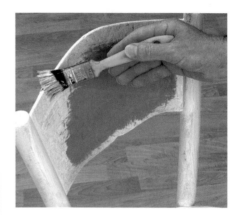

STEP 1 Give the old paintwork a good rub down with sandpaper, not removing all the paint but scratching the surface to provide a key for the primer. Apply a coat of white primer.

STEP 2 Apply one or two coats of the green top coat. If your upholstery fabric has green in the pattern, then try to match the chair colour to it. Use satin or eggshell paint or emulsion paint with a protective coat of varnish.

HOW TO DO IT: THE CUSHION/SEAT COVER

Choose a fabric that will look good with the rosy wall, something genuinely old or an offcut of soft furnishing fabric in a floral chintz. If the chair has a drop-in seat, remove it and use the seat itself as a template for the fabric. If you are making a loose cushion, follow the instructions below.

Round cushions are simple to make but the stitching must be done slowly to keep to the curve. A feather-filled round cushion pad is ideal for a bedroom chair.

STEP 1 Cut out two matching round pieces of fabric, adding a 50mm (2in) seam allowance all round the edges.

STEP 2 Pin the pieces together, right sides facing, leaving an opening for the cushion pad. If you would like a lace frill or piped edge then this has to be inserted and pinned at the same time.

STEP 3 Sew around the pinned seam line. Notch a seam allowance all round the cushion, then turn it the right way around.

STEP 4 Place the cushion pad inside the cover and neatly slip-stitch the opening.

Pure Romany

COLOUR
PALETTE

Romany style is most suited to people who prefer to keep one foot in the past and whose idea of bliss is a country kitchen with a cooking range. Rich, dark background colours are decorated using the light touch of single free-hand brushstrokes, with each pattern being composed of a mixture of stripes, swirls, dots and curves. Romany inspiration comes from the countryside and nature; flowers are the most popular decorative motif. Red, green, black and white are the main colours, but many other colours can be used for the decoration.

The colours explode with all the fun of the fair. Bright canal barges, decks piled high with vividly patterned tinware, fairground stalls and painted gypsy caravans are the inspiration for this look. Painting patterns were handed down through Romany families, and as lifestyles changed many of the traditional skills have disappeared. Fortunately the lazy, slow, canal-boat lifestyle appealed to people looking for an escape route from the fast pace of modern life, and since the Seventies many canal boats have been restored and brought back to their former vivid beauty. The main patterns used include flowers, leaves, castles, bridges, horses, playing cards, scallops and striped bands of colour. Lettering is often part of the design, spelling out the name of the barge or its owner.

Free style

If the idea of living in a painted horse-drawn caravan or a canal boat sounds appealing but impractical, then why not settle for bringing some of the colour and atmosphere into your home? The bright colours are set against a dark background of either black, dark green or blue, and all the patterns are painted free-

hand. It is a true peasant painting style, which is great fun to do as it requires the type of loose, confident brush stroke that is best achieved after a glass or two of wine!

If you love the patterns but find the brilliance of the colours too overwhelming, try artificially fading them with a milky glaze of varnish tinted with a small amount of white. This effect will be more like an old sun-bleached painted caravan needing a fresh coat of paint. If this appeals, then you could take the illusion a stage further and rub back some of the paint to simulate wear and tear.

Small is beautiful

On a large scale this would be quite overpowering, but it is perfect for a small cubby-hole of a room, or just as part of a room. These two projects show how to build and paint a pelmet and make curtains to hang below it. The window treatment will look equally good as the focal point in quite a plain room, as one of many patterns in a busy kitchen, or to add a touch of fantasy in a child's playroom. And a painted window-box filled with flowers outside the window is the perfect finishing touch.

PURE ROMANY: PROJECT ONE
A painted wooden pelmet

YOU WILL NEED:

A length of 150mm x 25mm (6in x 1in) shelving plank (measure the width of the window plus 100mm/4in)

Shelf brackets

A straight edge with a level

Drill

Masonry bit and wall plugs

Screws for the brackets

A length of hardboard 150mm (6in) wide or 6mm MDF – enough for boxing in the two ends and the length of the front

Hardboard pins

Small hammer

White chalk pencil

Black basecoat plus a selection of acrylic colours

Small decorator's brush

Artist's lining (long-haired) paintbrushes (fine, medium and broad)

Curtain rod and 2 end fittings

COLOUR KEY

1 Scarlet
2 Deep sage green
3 Leaf green
4 Black

A pelmet like this will look best fitted above a medium- to small-sized window. It is really easy to make, being basically a shelf on brackets with a strip of hardboard pinned onto the front and sides.

Pelmets are not very fashionable at the moment but do suit a folksy, traditional project like this, and the combination of pelmet and curtains makes a bold Romany-style statement.

One other bonus of making a pelmet is that it creates another shelf in the kitchen and provides a perfect place to display painted plates, jugs or even a vase of flowers.

TEMPLATE

These patterns are the outline shapes for the freehand painting. Either practise by copying them freehand or enlarge the patterns to the desired size and trace their outlines onto the pelmet. Do this by rubbing the back with chalk or using a chalk transfer paper.

HOW TO DO IT

Make a simple pelmet out of MDF or hardboard, paint it black and cover it with colourful Romany patterns.

STEP 1 Mark the pelmet position 50mm (2in) above the window recess. Check that it is straight using the spirit level, and draw a pencil line. Mark the screw positions for the shelf brackets on the wall and on the shelf plank.

STEP 2 Drill all the necessary holes, insert wall plugs and fix the brackets to the wall.

STEP 3 Cut the end pieces from the length of hardboard, then lay all three pieces flat and apply the basecoat. Leave to dry then apply a second coat.

STEP 4 Roughly mark out the pattern with the chalk pencil. Avoid using a ruler – use strips of paper as measuring guides where you need them.

STEP 5 Paint all the bands of colour and leave them to dry. Practise the base patterns on paper first, and when your hand has loosened up move on to paint the pattern details.

STEP 6 Paint as much decoration as you like, then fix the hardboard to the shelf front and sides. Screw the rod fittings into the inside ends. Use a small brush to touch up any pinheads or exposed edges, then fix the pelmet to the brackets.

PURE ROMANY: PROJECT TWO
Making felt appliqué curtains

COLOUR PALETTE

1
2
3
4
5

YOU WILL NEED:

Cotton drill:
2 x double the
window width
x the height plus
100mm (4in)

Felt in 4 other colours
(for example, green,
white, black, yellow)

Buttons for
decoration

Thread

Lining fabric – can be
cotton sheeting

Sewing machine

Rufflette tape for
curtain headings

Curtain rings

Fabric glue

A brush

COLOUR KEY

1 Leaf green
2 Scarlet
3 Deep sage green
4 Cream
5 Black

Felt decorations can give curtains a stylish, brightly coloured Romany look. Felt pattern shapes can be cut out and stuck down with glue. Although felt does not wash well, the colours are bright and will stay fresh-looking for a couple of years. The curtains are backed with a plain cotton lining.

Romany style has always included a variety of textiles – hand-dyed, woven, embroidered and appliquéed. The main pattern theme is a flower treated in a stylised way. These floral patterns are taken from Eastern European folk art and arranged in a typical way for decorating a long skirt or an apron.

TEMPLATE

Draw these patterns or copy them (enlarged to the desired size) and cut them out of thin paper. Then pin the patterns to felt and cut out the shapes.

HOW TO DO IT

These curtains are lined and headed with a simple tape and curtain rings. The decoration is glued in place with strong fabric glue but could also be fixed in place using a contrasting blanket stitch.

STEP 1 Cut out all the curtain and lining lengths. Draw the pattern shapes and cut them out of the coloured felt.

STEP 2 Arrange the pattern shapes on the background then glue each one in position (if you like hand sewing then these can be edged in contrasting running stitch or blanket stitch)

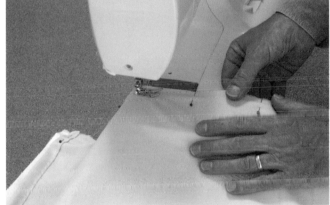

STEP 3 Turn over a narrow hem on the lining side seams, then pin the linings on to the front of the curtains along the top edge, allowing roughly 25mm (1in) for the seam. Stitch then turn the lining over onto the back and press the top seam flat.

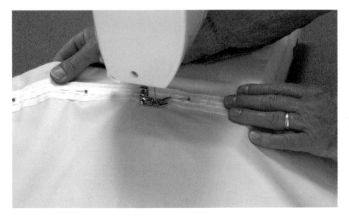

STEP 4 Pin the heading tape to the lining about 25mm (1in) from the top edge, then stitch it using the same colour thread as the felt curtain so that the stitching is invisible on the front.

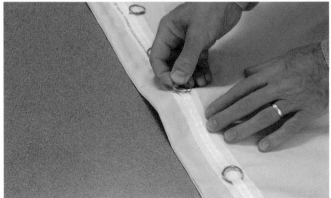

STEP 5 Fit the curtain rings onto the heading tape and hang the curtains from the rail. Pin up the hem with the lining tucked into the seam, then loosely slip-stitch the hem (this can be done without taking the curtains down.)

Provençal

Provence in the south of France has a wonderful climate, perfect light and stunning scenery. The Mediterranean sea and sky provide a vibrant blue background for the old buildings with their tall windows, balconies, shutters and awnings. Palm trees line the coast and the countryside is rocky and rugged, peppered with bushes of wild lavender, thyme and rosemary. There are olive groves and citrus orchards on the hillsides, and purple fields of lavender in the valleys. Yellow mimosa trees with their feathery leaves are everywhere.

Provence is a mixture of extreme wealth and high fashion in the popular Mediterranean coastal resorts of Nice and Cannes, co-existing alongside a traditional rustic lifestyle in the hills. Marseilles, France's main port, has a large population of North Africans, who have brought their own culture and decorative traditions with them. The regional style in Provence can be compared to a busy marketplace where many delicious influences converge and where the overwhelming feeling is that life is good.

Landscape colours

The predominant colours used for decorating are those that appear in the landscape – a range of earthy yellows and red browns used with bright blues and viridian greens. Terracotta is always there too, as clay plant pots and the rippling patterns of sun-bleached tiled rooftops. Walls are often painted using two colours, a deep shade below with a lighter one above. The bright sun soon fades exterior paintwork producing soft, muted, harmonious shades. Houses are decorated to feel cool inside, with tiled floors and pale-coloured walls.

Typically Provençal

Green is popular for its cooling effect, and ferns are the favourite house-plant. The wall-painting style is often quite rustic, rough and distressed in contrast to elaborate decorative wrought iron, stained glass, carved or painted furniture, lace curtains and richly patterned colourful fabrics. The distinctively complex Provençal floral and paisley fabric style is based on old Indian patterns brought back to Marseilles by sailors returning from the East in the 18th century. The French version of the fabric is still produced in the region, although the old handblocking and vegetable dyes have largely been replaced by modern textile printing methods and inks.

In a typical kitchen there will always be some colourful printed fabric, perhaps as a tablecloth or place mats. Displays of colourfully decorated plates and enamelware line the walls and shelves. Large cupboards, known as armoires, with wire mesh and gathered fabric door panels, are favoured over the modern fitted kitchen. Herbs hang from racks, vases are filled with flowers and the smell of coffee hangs in the air. C'est magnifique!

PROVENÇAL: PROJECT ONE
A painted kitchen table and chair

COLOUR PALETTE

1

2

3

YOU WILL NEED:

A pine table

A wooden kitchen chair

Sandpaper

Household bleach

Scrubbing brush

Protective goggles

Rubber gloves

Yellow paint

Pattern for chair-back drawn on transfer paper

Pencil

Tubes of pale and deep blue paint for detail (acrylic)

Household paintbrush (50mm/2in)

Artist's paintbrushes (one medium and one fine)

COLOUR KEY

1 Yellow-green
2 Mustard yellow
3 French blue

P reparing meals and eating together form a central part of the Provençal lifestyle, with the kitchen table at the heart of everything. For this project a plain pine table is given a new, more decorative French style with a scrubbed top and painted legs, and the wooden kitchen chair has been given a new coat of bright yellow paint and the finishing touch of a typical French Provençal motif. Look out for a country-style kitchen chair with a shapely backrest and, if you're very lucky, a rush seat. Some peeling paint or chipped enamelware is part of this look, and will give the room a sense of history.

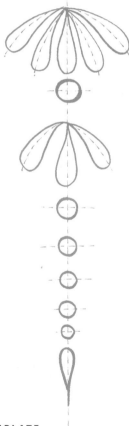

TEMPLATE
Trace this pattern twice to use across the back of a chair with an extra dot between them. Chalky backed transfer paper is ideal for this task and can be bought from art shops.

HOW TO DO IT
Give a pine table some character with a scrubbed top and brightly painted legs and paint a wooden chair to match.

STEP 1 Prepare the table legs and the chair for painting by sanding away any loose paint or varnish. Sand the top to remove all traces of varnish, then scrub it thoroughly with a 50/50 solution of bleach and water. Protect your eyes with goggles.

STEP 2 Apply a coat of primer, then two coats of yellow paint to the table legs and top rails.

STEP 3 Prime the chair, then apply two coats of yellow paint. Emulsion is used here for a matt finish, but gloss could be used instead for an easy-clean surface.

STEP 4 Trace the pattern twice to make a symmetrical pattern for the chair-back. Insert transfer paper between pattern and chair.

STEP 5 Tape the transfer paper and the pattern onto the chair-back. Go over the pattern in pencil.

STEP 6 Paint the pattern on the chair-back using free-flowing brushstrokes and two different sized brushes.

PROVENÇAL: PROJECT TWO
Tablecloth and napkins

YOU WILL NEED:

Fabric for the
tablecloth and
6 napkins: 2.25m of
1.2m width fabric
(90in of 48in
width fabric)

12m (13 yards) of
contrasting
rick-rack braid

Thread

Pins

Scissors

Sewing machine

The French lifestyle revolves around mealtimes, and in the south the lunch table is likely to be spread with one of the locally produced bright floral cloths. Square tablecloths and napkins are easy to make – all you need is a suitable piece of fabric and a border trimming. Genuine handblocked Provençal fabric can be bought in specialist stores, but there are many machine-printed versions. Better still, take a holiday in Provence and bring back the real thing! The trim used here is called rick-rack, but colour co-ordinated cotton fringe would also look good around the tablecloth.

COLOUR KEY

1 Deep Shaker blue

2 Bright orange

3 Sunshine yellow

HOW TO DO IT

This is sewing at its simplest and the most effort will involve getting the sewing machine set up.

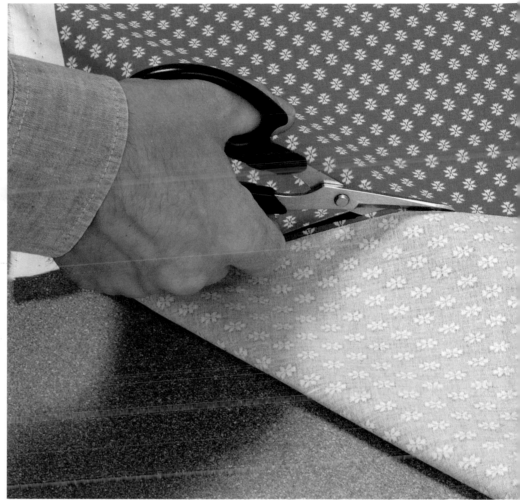

STEP 1 Cut out the square tablecloth by taking one corner of the fabric across to meet the other side. Align the edges, smooth the triangle flat and cut the fabric using the top edge as a guide. This will produce an accurate square.

STEP 2 Divide the remaining fabric into six 250mm (10in) squares.

STEP 3 Fold over a narrow hem on the cloth and napkins, and pin then machine them using zigzag stitch.

STEP 4 Pin the trimming around the edges of all the pieces and topstitch in a matching thread. Use a straight stitch and pay special attention to folding in the trimming ends, otherwise they could fray.

Tuscany

COLOUR PALETTE

Tuscany in summer presents the perfect antidote to a grey winter spent in a city – the effect is instantaneous and unforgettable. Italy, like every other industrialised society, has moved away from old-style farming and many Italians choose new, problem-free housing with all mod cons over the tumbledown old farm buildings that fire the visitor's imagination. The restoration of farmhouses and villas in the Tuscan countryside has largely been undertaken by outsiders, for whom it was a case of 'love at first sight'.

It seems that another culture's rural lifestyle always has more appeal than one's own, doubly so when the weather is good. The outsiders have rescued what the locals would have thrown out in the name of progress, and craftsmen have found their traditional skills in great demand.

Tuscany has a treasury of art, architecture and culture in cities such as Florence and Siena, where the climate has helped to preserve its beauty. The colours of marble, earth and clay predominate, with the sun playing its part by fading fresh paint to blend seamlessly with the colours of older buildings.

The Tuscan climate is hot and dry, and houses are built of local stone with curved earthenware roof tiles. Windows have wooden shutters and the colouring of the buildings allows them to blend into the landscape.

Simple and functional

Inside, the houses have tiled floors and plastered walls painted in pink, shades of faded blue green or ochre yellow. There are no skirting boards, but the lower part of the walls are painted in a darker colour to hide the scuff marks made by the broom.

The small windows shield interiors from the scorching heat of the summer sun and the cold winter nights. Curtains are rare, but wooden shutters are fitted inside the windows, making it easy to block out the light during the afternoon rest hours. Windows ledges are tiled, and the broad bands surrounding windows and doorways are picked out in softly contrasting colours. The paint used in Tuscany is always limewash tinted with pigments. This is the perfect paint for the climate, and the chalky finish is essential for the authentic Tuscan look.

The furnishing style is simple and functional, as most entertaining takes place outside on the terrace. In Italy, furniture is often arranged against the walls rather than in the centre of a room to keep an open, spacious feeling. A few pieces of wooden furniture, some hand-painted ceramics, pot plants, Turkish rugs and table lamps are all in keeping with this style. Terracotta floor tiles are practical in an entrance hall and a kitchen, but are only suitable for living rooms in warmer climates. Polished floorboards and rugs look good and feel warmer underfoot.

The key to success is to keep it simple.

TUSCANY: PROJECT ONE
A small shuttered wall cupboard

YOU WILL NEED:

Timber (see Timber Requirements, right) plus small scrap of wood to make a catch

4 x hinges

1 x iron bolt

Small panel pins

Wood glue

Hammer

Handsaw

Screwdriver

Small screws

Bradawl

6 cup hooks

2 mirror fixings

Rust red paint

Paint brush

COLOUR KEY

1 Sea green

2 Rust red

3 Deep ochre

This shallow cupboard looks like a wooden shuttered window you would find in a farmhouse. On the wall in an entrance hall it creates the illusion of a window, when it is actually a key cupboard. Recycled timber gives the most rustic effect – or use part of a small louvred door.

The idea is to make a box with a decorative lid to hang on the wall. For the backing plate, use timber thick enough to allow for hooks to be screwed in. The traditional colours used for shuttered windows are red-brown or blue-green, both of which soon fade and mellow in the bright sunshine.

TEMPLATE

Draw a template based on these designs. The cupboard made here is 290mm x 330mm x 25mm, but adapt your template to the size you require.

TIMBER REQUIREMENTS

back: 290mm x 330mm (11½in x 13in)

sides : 2 x 25mm x 25mm (1in x 1in), measuring 290mm (11½in);

top/bottom: 2 x 25mm x 25mm (1in x 1in), measuring 285mm (11¼

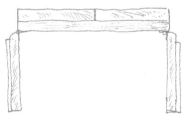

doors: 140mm x 325mm (5½in x 12½in)

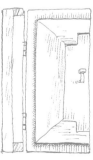

panelling:
70mm wide x 290mm long mitred (2¾in x 11½in);
70mm wide x 125mm long mitred (2¾in x 4⅞in)

HOW TO DO IT

This idea can be adapted to suit your needs or the timber you have available. The cupboard is simply glued and pinned together.

Step 1 Cut all the pieces to size (see Timber Requirements, opposite). Sand as necessary.

Step 2 Make up the shallow box with simple butt joints, using wood glue and panel pins to secure the sides and fix them to the back.

Step 3 Make up the two front doors, adding extra panels and cross bars to give the shutter style (if required).

Step 4 Attach the doors to the box base using two hinges for each door.

Step 5 Fix the iron bolt onto the front to joint the doors in the middle.

Step 6 Apply two coats of paint. When the cupboard is dry, screw six hooks (or more) into the back of it, then fit the mirror fixings onto the back and fix the cupboard onto the wall.

TUSCANY: PROJECT TWO
A painted wall finish

COLOUR
PALETTE

YOU WILL NEED:

Three shades of chalk-finish paint

Large paintbrush suitable for colourwashing

Paint kettle

Masking tape

Long rule with spirit level

Pencil for marking the wall

The Tuscan decorating style is a simple one that uses weathered, textured and harmonious colour with no hard lines, startling primary colours or sharp contrasts. The look is not difficult to reproduce with Mediterranean paint that dries to a chalky finish. A slightly textured wall surface and colourwashed effect will intensify the Tuscan flavour, and the rough texture can be effectively applied with a special textured paint in a sand or farmhouse finish. The colour here is also used to surround the small key cupboard to add to the illusion of it being a shuttered window.

COLOUR KEY

1 Deep ochre
2 Dark terracotta
3 Deep purple

HOW TO DO IT

Keep the brush strokes fresh and energetic and use chalky water-based paint for an authentic Tuscan wall finish.

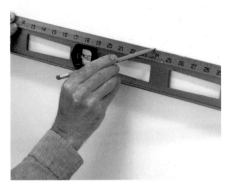

STEP 2 Measure 1m (3ft) up from the floor and mark the wall at intervals. Draw a line along the length of the wall.

STEP 1 Measure a border of 100mm (4in) around any window, doorway or fitted feature, such as a cupboard, and mark this in pencil.

STEP 3 Place masking tape on the lower side of the 1m (3ft) line and inside the border line.

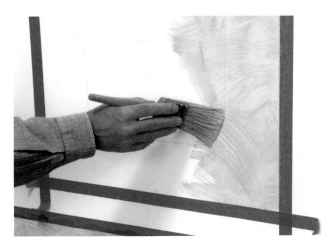

STEP 4 Dilute the paint and apply it to the lower wall and inside the inner border for the feature using random brushstrokes. Then leave it to dry.

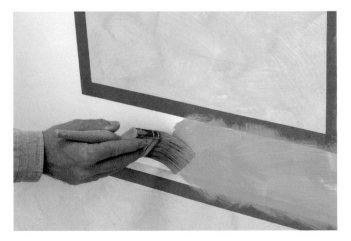

STEP 5 Renew the tape and paint the top part of the wall and the outer border of the feature using the second, diluted paint. Peel off the tape and paint a freehand stripe in terracotta across the wall.

Moorish casbah

The Moorish style comes from the north of Africa where Morocco nestles between the Atlas mountains and the sea. This meeting point of African and Muslim culture has a rich artistic and cultural tradition. Islamic art and decoration is based on geometric patterns as the religion forbids the making of images. Houses are built around inner courtyards with plain, fortress-style exteriors; all of the decoration is on the inside. The courtyards are lined with open balconies, often with rows of columns and elaborate arches.

One of the most stunning features in Moorish homes is the tiling. Tiles are used on walls and floors to create elaborate interwoven shapes and patterns. The star features in most patterns, usually in the centre of a radiating trellis-work of star patterns. The main colours used are blue, white, black, pale green and terracotta. Colours are jewel-bright, whether on walls, tiles or woven in textiles.

Domes and arches

Other important features in Moorish design are domes, arches and water. Doorways are arched and windows are usually covered with decorative metal grilles. Walled rooftop terraces are the most popular place for evening entertaining. Walls are either topped off with stepped patterns or simply castellated and whitewashed to reflect the searing heat. Pools and fountains cool the courtyards, and date palms provide shade.

Pierced lanterns, leather pouffes, carved tea tables and intricately woven rugs are typical furnishings. Low couches are spread with rugs and silk cushions in all shapes and sizes. It is a style that encourages relaxation and a more exotic, sensual way of living.

Moroccan style is not expensive or beyond our reach thanks to the market culture which exists at the source in Morocco and in all major cities in Europe. The hippy trail led straight to Marrakesh in the late 1960s, and people soon discovered that they could finance their nomadic lifestyles by buying Moroccan goods and selling them back home to fund their next visit. As a result, the markets were flooded with folding tables, rugs, lanterns, trays and ceramics, many of which can still be picked up at reasonable prices in flea markets today. The ethnic decorating style which has been popular recently has brought a new wave of stylish Moroccan imports, but there are also plenty of beautiful and inexpensive pierced tin lanterns, sets of tea glasses, textiles and rugs on offer through homestyle stores and mail order catalogues.

Exuberant palette

Travel guides for the area and books on Moorish architecture and interiors show this to be a rich mixture of sophisticated building and decoration enhanced by an exuberant ethnic palette.

MOORISH CASBAH: PROJECT ONE
A painted arch bedhead

YOU WILL NEED:

Deep-blue chalky
finish paint

Pink paint

Deep terracotta paint

2 x 100mm (4in)
squares of thick foam

Star pattern template

Scalpel

Spraymount

Brown wrapping
paper for the arch
template

Scissors

Chalk

Large brush to apply
main colour

Small paintbrush
for edges

3

COLOUR KEY

1 Tangerine
2 Deep ultramarine
3 Palest lemon

Turn your bedroom into a scene from
A Thousand and One Nights by painting
the walls a warm pink stone colour and
painting a typically Moorish arch at the
bedhead in deep ultramarine blue with a
stamped tile surround. Enhance the kasbah
atmosphere with metal lanterns, candles, urns
and striped woven textiles. All the other
colours in the room should be rich and warm
so that the effect is one of looking up at an
inky blue Moroccan night sky. If this effect
appeals to you, why not go one step further
and paint a distant sickle moon and stars on
the blue arch shape?

TEMPLATE

Draw the star pattern so that it fits
neatly into a 100mm (4in) square
following the method shown in
the diagram.

HOW TO DO IT

This arched bedhead does not take long to paint, and the stamped tiles are simple, bold and effective.

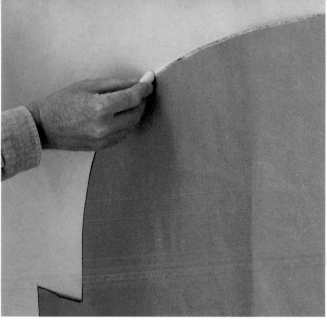

STEP 1 Enlarge and draw one half of the arch pattern onto the brown parcel paper, either in sections on a photocopier or by squaring up. Cut it out and spray a light coating of Spraymount on one side.

STEP 2 Stick this onto the wall and draw the shape with chalk, then flip the template over and repeat these steps to create a complete arch.

STEP 3 Enlarge the star pattern to 80mm (3⅛in) wide and stick the pattern onto one of the foam squares. Carefully cut out the shape to the depth of about 15mm (⅝in). Cut outwards from the middle every time. Peel off the background to 15mm (⅝in), leaving a star-shaped stamp.

STEP 4 Paint the arch in deep blue, using the small brush for a neat finish around the edges.

STEP 5 Put some of the terracotta paint onto a plate and coat the square tile stamp. Stamp a tile border around the edge of the arch, leaving the top triangle for now. Allow to dry.

STEP 6 Now coat the star stamp in pink and place one star in every tile shape. Cut a foam stamp in a triangle shape to fill the gap at the top and on each side where the arch meets the straight supporting column. Fill in the gaps with this stamp using the terracotta colour.

MOORISH CASBAH: PROJECT TWO
Mosaic mirror frame

COLOUR
PALETTE

1'

2

3

4

YOU WILL NEED:

12mm (½in) plywood base 400mm x 250mm (16in x 10in)

12mm (½in) plywood frame pieces, 2 x 50mm x 350mm (2in x 14in) and 2 x 50mm x 200mm (2in x 8in)

Mirror, cut to size

Wood glue and clamps

Tile adhesive and terracotta-tinted grout

Mosaic tesserae

Mosaic snippers

PVA adhesive

Brush

Mirror fixings and screws

Tiling is very much a part of the Moorish style, and a mirror framed with tiles will look perfect in this setting. If you have never made a mosaic before, then this is the project to start with. Mosaic is not difficult, and there is always a wonderful surprise at the end when the grouting is wiped off and the bright jewel colours are revealed. Choose colours that would appear in Moroccan tiling such as blue, white, orange and black, and either adapt an existing frame or make a new one one from plywood with a raised beading edge. A cut-down border of tiles around the inside edge of the mirror creates the illusion of depth.

COLOUR KEY

1 Light leaf green

2 Turquoise

3 Pure orange

4 Tangerine

HOW TO DO IT

Begin by making a simple plywood backing with a wide frame stuck on it as a recess for a mirror. Mosaic tiles are then arranged, stuck and grouted to stunning effect.

STEP 1 Glue the frame pieces onto the base as shown, then clamp and leave until the glue has bonded. Outline the pattern on the frame in pencil.

STEP 2 Lay out the pattern, gluing each piece as you go. This is a very simple pattern and you should not need to trim any of the pieces.

STEP 3 When the frame pattern is laid, glue the mirror into the middle with a large squiggle of glue.

STEP 4 You may need to cut tiles to fit into the area between the mirror and the surface of the mosaic. Glue uncut tesserae to the outside edge of the frame so that they align with the surface of the mosaic. Grout the mosaic, making sure that the grout fills all the gaps, then polish the tiles and mirror with a soft cloth.

India

COLOUR PALETTE

The subcontinent of India is a huge country of many distinct characters. The Buddhist north is mountainous with a cold climate, and to the west lie the farmlands and deserts of Rajasthan and Gujarat, which border the Arabian Sea. The Hindu south has the hottest climate and the most relaxed lifestyle, and here the economy is based around the traditional creative industries of textile printing and carving. The east has the River Ganges, jungles, mangrove swamps and Calcutta, the most overpopulated city in India.

There is no such thing as one Indian style, but one thing all the regions have in common is that they mix brilliant colours in ways that break all the Western rules defining 'good taste' and colour combining! The result is vibrant, energising and uniquely Indian. Colours are flung together with great confidence, and their impact is stunning. Different areas of India are famous for their skills in specific crafts such as embroidery, textile printing, pottery or carpet weaving, but there is no area where most of these traditional skills are not practised anyway.

Brilliant work

It is clear from the dress, homes and jewellery of the craftspeople who produce these items that they have a genuine love for the patterns, colours and motifs they reproduce, even though they are poorly paid for the work that they do. Most of the work is produced for the home market. Houses in cities are painted in brilliant colours; temples are adorned with carvings and bronze castings, and each festival generates a hive of industry producing all the necessary deities, offerings and accessories needed for a proper celebration.

Seeking out the style

Many of the styles we recognise as our own have their origins in India. The paisley shawl, floral chintz, Madras check, Provençal prints and damask cottons all came from India. Several charities now have Fair Trade arrangements with communities of craftspeople in India who supply goods directly for sale in their high street shops, so it is really easy to buy genuine handmade accessories, textiles and ornaments to give a room the right feel.

The sari stores found in the local shops of Asian communities sell lengths of fabric ranging from plain vibrant muslins for everyday wear to the finest exquisitely embroidered cloth for wedding saris. Sari lengths are ideal for draping over curtain poles at windows or as exotic drapes for a four-poster bed.

Most paint companies produce vibrant colour ranges. Choose the mainstream emulsion paints for children's rooms where these brilliant colour schemes will always find an appreciative audience; or buy a Mediterranean-style paint that dries to leave an authentic powdery bloom.

INDIA: PROJECT ONE
Wall painting with borders

YOU WILL NEED:

Chalk for marking
up the wall

A long rule and spirit
level

Brilliant pink
emulsion paint

Blue violet emulsion
paint

Red emulsion paint

Paint roller and tray

Small paint roller
and tray

50mm (2in)
paintbrush

COLOUR KEY

1 Purple
2 Shell pink
3 Soft violet
4 Rose pink

Brilliant pink is very typically Indian, especially when seen with crimson red and blue violet. Saris have bands of decoration at each end, and this is the source of inspiration for the project. The border edges are painted free-hand – don't worry if it waves and wanders a bit, as it will look softer that way. To carry on the Indian theme, drape a real sari at the window as a curtain with a beaded necklace or belt for a tie back. Indian trinket boxes, ornaments, brightly coloured woven baskets and rugs can all be bought from stores that specialise in ethnic goods.

HOW TO DO IT

Take time to measure and mark the wall before applying each colour. The small foam roller is just the right width for the border and creates a nice soft edge to the stripe.

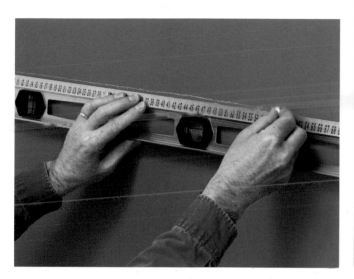

STEP 1 Measure and mark the wall at 750mm (30in) and 1m (3ft) height from the floor. Mark all the way around the walls, then draw lines in chalk – use a dark colour for light walls.

STEP 2 Paint the top section of the wall first, using the roller to apply the bright pink colour. If you overlap the guide line, wait for the paint to dry then re-draw the chalk line.

STEP 3 Move to the lowest section, which can also include the skirting board. If the wood has been painted with gloss it should be rubbed down or primed with an all-surface primer prior to painting. Paint this section red and leave to dry.

STEP 4 Use the small foam roller with the blue-violet paint and carefully paint a band of colour between the red and the pink.

INDIA: PROJECT TWO

Bindi stamps and a border stamp

YOU WILL NEED:

High density foam

Scalpel

Copies of the patterns

Spraymount

Size (special glue)

Small foam roller

Plumb line marked at 300mm (12in) intervals.

2 or more packs of gold leaf – (the squares can be cut in half with scissors or a scalpel, to avoid waste)

COLOUR KEY

1 Deep lavender

2 Lilac

3 Lavender grey

4 Palest lemon

5 Apricot

Very few textiles escape having some extra form of decoration beyond colour dye in India. It is as if they simply cannot resist adding another pattern, thread or ornament.

These little teardrop shapes are inspired by the decorative marks which Indian women paint or apply to their foreheads, called bindi.

The shape is stamped onto the wall using a clear glue called gold size, then when it is almost dry a sheet of gold leaf is rubbed over it. The result is a gleaming gold shape. The pattern for the border is larger and can be applied either in the same way or with a bright pink paint colour as shown here.

TEMPLATE

These are the actual size patterns for the foam stamps and can be traced from the book. Use thin paper that will be easily cut through when you make the stamps.

HOW TO DO IT

Foam stamps can be made from any firm foam,
but cutting needs to be done slowly and accurately
to get the best effect.

STEP 1 Make copies of the patterns and stick them on the foam. Cut them out carefully, using a scalpel. Practise cutting on an off-cut to judge how much pressure is needed. Cut at an angle so the base of the pattern is wider than the top; this makes the stamp stronger.

STEP 2 Put 1 tablespoon of size on a plate and run the foam roller through it. Coat the bindi and stamp it onto the wall at 600mm (25in) intervals using the plumb line as a guide. Stamp the next row, starting 300mm (12in) from the ceiling to make a half-drop pattern.

STEP 3 Take a sheet of gold leaf with its backing sheet and rub it gently onto the stamped size. The leaf will cling to the size, but easily brush away from the surrounding wall. Don't worry if the motifs are not sharp-edged – this is typical of the hand-blocked style.

STEP 4 Apply size to the border stamp and repeat the pattern along the deep violet band. Complete the whole length of the wall, then apply the sheets of gold leaf. Brush away the excess, then burnish the gold with a soft cloth.

African

The African continent is one of many contrasts, divided in half at the equator by a band of heavy forests. To the north is the massive Sahara desert with the huge countries of Egypt and Sudan. Egypt is one of the great ancient civilizations, whose past is well documented compared to the other African civilizations. In contrast, there are still tribes who lead a Stone Age existence as hunter-gatherers deep in the equatorial forests, or as nomadic huntsmen in the Southern deserts.

East Africa borders the Indian Ocean and the Red Sea, and trade with India and the Arab countries over the centuries has made North East Africa more Arab in style than African. There are white domed buildings, minarets, date palms and bustling markets. Southern Africa has the grasslands, lakes, mountains and semi-deserts, and wildlife, and people traditionally lived off the land as herdsmen and farmers. Much of Africa's rich heritage of art, crafts and architecture was undermined by colonization, and only recently has a pride in true African style re-emerged.

Updated traditions

The textiles of West Africa are amazingly varied. Traditional fabric patterns were tie-dyed or patterned using the mud-resist technique, and coloured with indigo or other organic plant dyes. Modern dyes are used now, with mixtures of old and new designs. Some of the most interesting feature objects such as bicycles or clocks as design motifs set within traditional border patterns. Utility objects such as baskets, rugs or pottery remain unchanged. Authentic African goods including textiles and household goods have

been added to beadwork, trinkets and wood carvings for the export market. The abstract patterns and simple shapes fit in well with contemporary interiors.

African colour

The Southern African colour palette comes from the earth. Red ochre, yellow, burnt orange and black dominate, with any other available colour used to riotous effect. In some places telephone wires are split open and the multi-colour wires used to weave baskets; in others tin cans are recycled to make storage trunks, lamps and toys.

Creating an authentic African-style room should not be difficult or expensive. The look is simple and relies on a few well-chosen objects, shapes and colours. The walls are roughly textured and painted in bands of colour, dark at the bottom and light above. Patterns are loosely geometric and rhythmic. There are specialist stores that deal in African furniture and crafts; baskets, masks, woven wall hangings and soapstone carvings are always on sale in Oxfam's stores and it is always worth exploring flea markets and junk shops for stools, tables or curios.

AFRICAN: PROJECT ONE

African walls

YOU WILL NEED:

Earthy orange, golden yellow, mud brown and warm terracotta paints in sample size for stencilling

Matt black emulsion paint (small tin)

Short-pile roller

Broad paintbrush

40mm (1½in) paintbrush

Long rule and spirit level

Pencil

Stencil card

Spraymount

Scalpel

Short, fat stencil brush

The walls in African homes have undulating surfaces that are pitted and rough in places and shiny smooth in others. Smooth walls may need roughing up a bit to achieve the African look. There are several ways to do this. The least expensive is to apply a skim coat of plaster with a wooden trowel, but this is something of a specialist job. A thin, uneven coat of filler can be applied, with a plastering trowel or a large brush, having mixed it 50:50 into white emulsion paint; or special effect paint, applied with a short-pile roller and given random criss-cross strokes with a decorating brush.

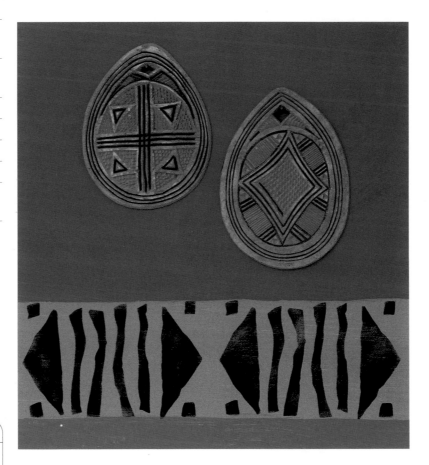

COLOUR KEY

1 Earthy orange
2 Golden yellow
3 Mud brown
4 Warm terracotta

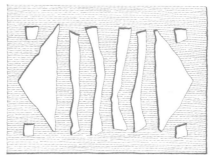

TEMPLATE
This stencil imitates stick printed patterns, so keep the lines irregular when you cut it out.

HOW TO DO IT

Stencilling is easy and effective so long as you use
Spraymount to hold the stencil in place and remember
to use only the smallest amount of paint on your brush.

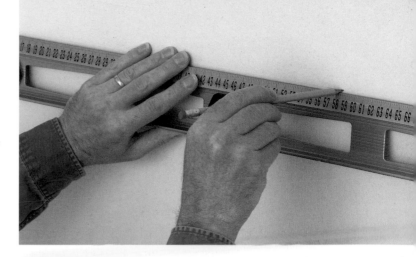

STEP 1 Measure and mark the wall at
750mm (30in) and 1m (3ft) height at 1m (3ft)
intervals around the walls and draw
guidelines for the three bands.

STEP 2 Paint the top and bottom parts of the wall first
and leave to dry.

STEP 3 Paint the dividing band with your chosen emulsion. Paint the
lines free-hand using the narrower brush along the edges and filling
in with the broader brush.

STEP 4 Cut out the stencil pattern and apply a small amount of
Spraymount to the back of it.

STEP 5 Stencil the pattern in the centre band in your chosen colour.

AFRICAN: PROJECT TWO
Cushion cover

YOU WILL NEED:

Large potato

Pattern

Sharp kitchen knife

Plate

Small foam roller or square-tipped paintbrush

Felt-tipped pen

Scalpel

Lino cutting tools (scoop and v-shape gouges)

Fabric printing ink

A plain cushion cover

Newspaper

The charm of this type of African textile pattern lies in the slight irregularities that are so much a part of the process of printing by hand.

This type of pattern would usually be stamped onto fabric using a carved wooden block, but this one is produced with a potato cut. Potato printing has a liberating, youthful quality, which is particularly well suited to the African style. The same pattern is quite versatile; here it is used in an all-over pattern for a cushion, but it could be used to make a border for curtains or a throw.

A potato stamp has a limited life but can be saved overnight in a jug of cold water then dried well before being used again.

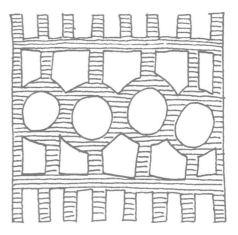

TEMPLATE
Draw the template to fit the surface of your halved potato.

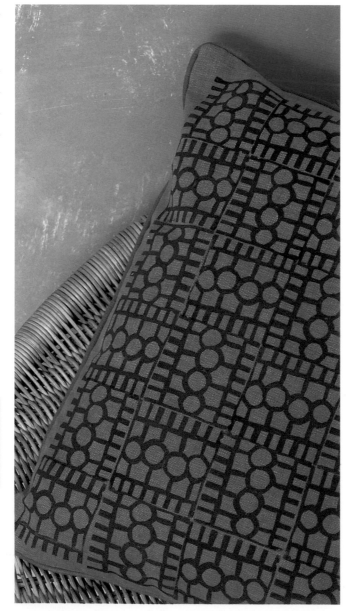

COLOUR KEY

1 Earthy orange

2 Warm terracotta

3 Deep red brown

4 Brick red

5 Cream

HOW TO DO IT

Potato printing is great fun but large potatoes can be tricky to hold. Cut out a notch on each side of the potato to make a handle, as shown in Step 4.

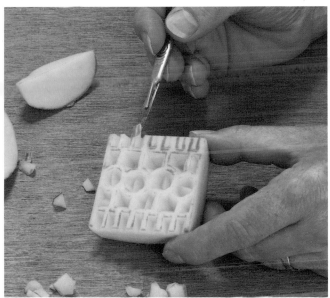

STEP 1 Cut the potato in half using the kitchen knife, and draw the motif onto the surface with the felt-tipped pen.

STEP 2 Cut around the motif edges using the scalpel, then scoop away all the background.

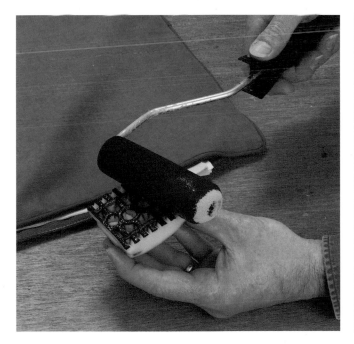

STEP 3 Put a padding of newspaper inside the cushion cover. Place some of the printing ink on the plate and use the foam roller or brush to coat the potato stamp. Stamp once or twice onto kitchen paper, then re-coat the stamp and stamp onto the fabric.

STEP 4 Stamp the pattern in rows, then iron to fix the ink following the manufacturer's instructions.

Scandinavian simplicity

The North European countries of Norway, Sweden, Denmark and Iceland are collectively known as Scandinavia. Much of the area lies inside the Arctic Circle, and the sea separates four of the countries from Mainland Europe. Although each country has preserved its own national identity, the similarities in climate, landscape and building materials make it possible to bind the regional differences together as Scandinavian style – bright colours on the outside, and cool, sophisticated colours on the inside.

Timber is Scandinavia's traditional building material, used both inside and out. The extensive pine forests provide a ready supply of construction timber, and country houses are still built in traditional styles and painted in vivid colour combinations. The colours used to decorate the outside are very likely to be stronger than those used on the inside. Houses painted rich brick red with bright blue, yellow ochre with sea green, or bright blue with yellow and white all rub happily up against each other. It is a practical solution in these cold, northern countries where the landscape is often snow covered and houses need to stand out to be seen.

City style

City buildings are much grander, built in an elegant, classically influenced style. Scandinavia was slow to become industrialised and therefore managed to avoid the chaotic frenzy of building that took place around most big cities. Having held back initially they were able to take a more structured, aspirational 'lifestyle' approach to the design of their towns. Their sophisticated exterior design awareness extended to the interior

design, incorporating furniture, glassware, ceramics and traditional crafts.

The Gustavian style is named after King Gustav III, who fell in love with English and French interiors in the late 18th century. In those days, what met with the King's approval became the fashion of the day, and Gustavian remains one of the most recognisably Scandinavian interior styles.

Minimalist meets traditional

Furniture is upholstered in soft blue or yellow checks; walls are pale blue, sometimes striped with white; floors are polished pale pine and elegant chandeliers provide the lighting. This style has found grace with people who admire the minimalist approach in principle, but still hark after a more traditional style of interior decorating. It combines the best of both worlds, being perceived as modern for its cool, calm, uncluttered style and limited colour palette, and traditional for the inclusion of accessories such as antique chandeliers and gilded mirrors,which are central to a successful Gustavian look.

Unclutter your life and try a little Scandinavian chic.

SCANDINAVIAN SIMPLICITY: PROJECT ONE

Easy wall stripes

YOU WILL NEED:

A white-painted wall

Small foam roller and tray (3 pack of rollers)

Plumb line

Pale blue emulsion paint

Pale grey emulsion paint

Small paintbrush

25mm (1in) masking tape

Scalpel

Hand-painted stripes, borders and panels are popular Scandinavian wall treatments. The more detailed patterns feature twisting ribbons, floral posies, bows and garlands, often painted in a naturalistic, three-dimensional style. This project shows how to paint broad stripes with a roller. The roller can be trimmed to make thin stripes for a more detailed pattern. Choose calm colours to complement the style, such as pale yellow and white or blue and white. The bold colours used in this large light and airy room might be overpowering in a small space; they could be toned down for a more subtle effect.

COLOUR KEY

1 Pure blue

2 Pale aqua

3 Blue-grey

4 Light sky blue

HOW TO DO IT

Painting stripes with a foam roller is easy, but there is a knack to getting the right amount of paint for a whole stripe and using the right pressure. Begin on a part of the room that will not be the focus of attention.

STEP 1 Fill the tray with blue paint and run the roller through so that it is evenly coated. Test this on paper first to judge the pressure needed for good coverage and no runs.

STEP 2 Hang the plumb line from ceiling height about 300mm (12in) in from one corner. Paint a stripe from ceiling to skirting. The roller leaves gaps at top and bottom that can be filled in with the paintbrush. Leave a roller's width between stripes and move the plumb line as you go.

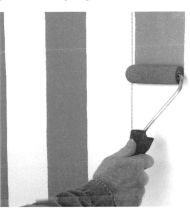

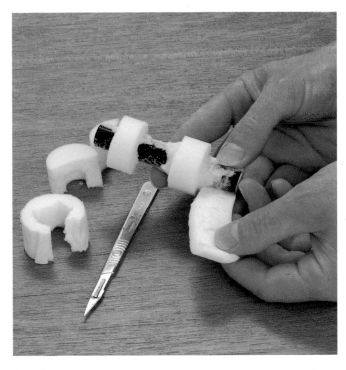

STEP 3 Divide up a new roller by wrapping masking tape around each end and the middle section. This will leave two foam pieces showing. Use a scalpel to cut down the edges of the tape and to remove the taped pieces. You will be left with two foam ridges.

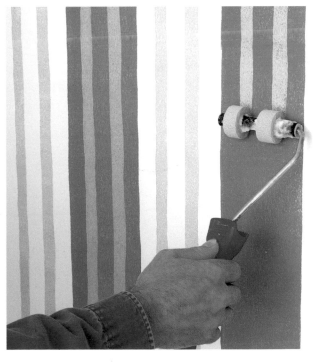

STEP 4 Fill the tray with grey paint and run the roller through it. Test the twin stripes on paper first. Run the roller down the white stripes and the blue stripes to add a double grey stripe. Fill in the small gaps at the top and bottom with the paintbrush.

SCANDINAVIAN SIMPLICITY: PROJECT TWO
A Scandinavian dining chair

FOR THE CHAIR YOU WILL NEED

A chair with a padded seat – either drop-in or fixed

Matt white paint

A candle

Paintbrush or small foam roller and tray

Sandpaper

FOR THE UPHOLSTERY YOU WILL NEED

Scissors

Striped or checked woven fabric (heavier than school dress gingham)

Staple gun

This project requires you to visit a few junk shops in search of a suitable chair to rescue. Look for a well proportioned wooden dining chair that could have a tall rounded or short square back and a drop-in seat. The shape should be elegant but not overly decorative. If you find one with a nice back and legs but a plain wooden seat, buy it and make a tie-on cushion in place of reupholstering the seat. A popular treatment for dining chairs in Sweden is to make small frilled skirted cushions. Strip away any old paint or varnish by hand or have it dipped professionally. Let it dry before re-painting.

HOW TO DO IT: THE CHAIR

Renovating a wooden chair is a very satisfying make-over project. The clean-up, painting and upholstery are all enjoyable, and the result can be remarkable. Take care to remove all traces of the old varnish and make repairs before you repaint.

STEP 1 Rub the edges of the chair-back and any raised pattern on the wood, the curve of the legs and the seat corners with the candle. A light stroke will be enough.

STEP 2 Apply two coats of the white paint, allowing the correct drying time in between and after.

STEP 3 Rub the waxed areas with sandpaper. The paint should lift away easily, so that the bare wood shows through in places. It is important not to overdo this effect as it is meant to simulate natural wear and tear.

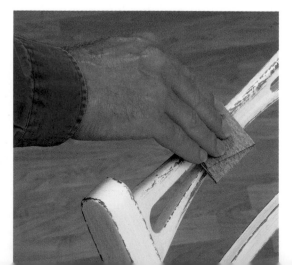

COLOUR KEY

1 Sunshine yellow
2 Ice blue
3 Violet

HOW TO DO IT: THE UPHOLSTERY

This is the simplest of all upholstery tasks – all you need is a pair of scissors, a stapler and a spare half hour. Discard any tatty old upholstery, but if the padding and cover are intact simply place the new one over the old.

STEP 1 Lay the seat face down on the lining fabric and cut out the shape, adding an extra 50mm (2in) on all sides to allow for the seat depth and turning under. Using this as a pattern, cut out the checked fabric.

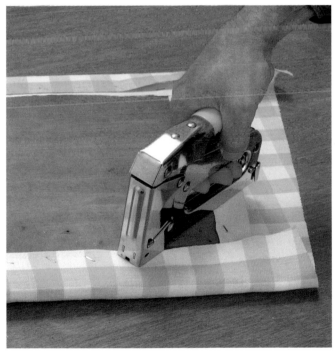

STEP 2 Lay the fabric face down on a flat surface with the seat on top. Pull it round to the back of the seat and staple half way along one side. Pull tight and staple the opposite side. Do the same with the other two opposite sides. Fold the corners over and staple them flat. Now pleat the fabric on each side of the corners and staple that down. Add several more staples along each side to secure the new cover. Drop the seat back into the frame.

Miami pastel brights

Miami Beach at the tip of Florida has a style all of its own. The resort was built between the 1920s and 1940s in the Art Deco style, which was popular in New York and Chicago, but in Miami they gave the look a unique twist by choosing a very different range of colours for their buildings. In Miami the buildings were painted with bright tropical pinks, sunny yellows, purples, blues and greens. The colours were not primaries but bright pastel ice cream colours, perfect for a holiday town.

The buildings echoed the shape of streamlined ocean liners, with the main body of the building painted white and colour used to highlight the horizontal banding. For a while Miami was the most glamorous holiday destination, but it fell on hard times in the late 1950s. In the 1980s a massive renovation plan was set in motion, and now Miami outshines its former glory. The buildings are freshly painted and are a little brighter, with less white and more entire buildings painted bright colours; the chrome is polished and neon signs light up the night. The interiors are decorated in a similar style, using colours to stress the geometric devices in the design such as columns, stepped parapets and windows with narrow horizontal glazing bars. Also synonymous with Miami are palm trees, tropical flowers, nautical themes, flamingos and unrestrained elegance.

Art Deco Miami-style

Miami is now one of the world's top holiday resorts, and its stylish hotels and boulevards are favourite locations for films and fashion photography. Creating your own piece of South Beach (SoBe) should not be too hard because a distinctive colour scheme will do most of the work for you. Look out for one or two genuine Art Deco pieces of furniture, either from specialist dealers or flea markets.

Miami used Art Deco shapes but applied its own colour scheme – you can do the same with bright pastel upholstery. If you have no luck finding original furniture, buy a plain sofa with a streamlined shape and dress it up with contrasting cushions piped in Miami colours.

A touch of fun

Neon lighting is very much a part of the Miami look, and a pair of coloured neon tubes would add an authentic glow at night. These can be bought as coloured sheaths to fit over standard tubes. Chrome wall or table lights will also fit in well, and there are plenty of good reproduction Art Deco lights around.

Miami has a fun side, and if this appeals to you then a fake flamingo or two and a few stylized sunset pictures are a must! In Miami, the sun shines all year and most residents are on permanent vacation. Adopt this style at home so that, even if work occupies the day, every evening will feel like a holiday.

MIAMI PASTEL BRIGHTS: PROJECT ONE

Miami deco walls

YOU WILL NEED:

Background colour (choose one of the three below) to apply to all wall surfaces first

Pink, yellow and sea green paint

Pencil

Long rule

Spirit level

Plumb line

Paintbrush

Roller and tray

Small foam roller and tray

Decorator's masking tape

The geometric and streamlined shapes associated with Art Deco can be used mural-style, drawn onto a wall and painted using the Miami palette of tropical bright pastels. The most important lines to emphasize are the horizontals, which should wrap around the room in smooth streamlined stripes. Vertical columns topped off with stepped parapets can be painted around doorways or windows.

Miami is very style-conscious but fun is also high on the agenda, so use the basic shapes and colours but feel free to interpret the style in your own way.

COLOUR PALETTE

1

2

3

COLOUR KEY

1 Lemon curd

2 Deep rose

3 Aqua blue

HOW TO DO IT

Wrapping your walls with these bands of Miami colour will liven up any room. It's fun, but don't rush it as the paint needs to be dry before you apply the tape.

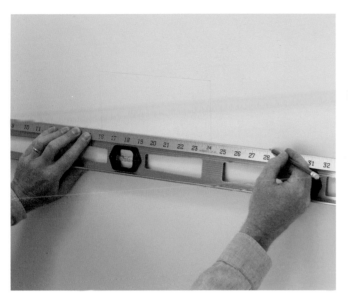

STEP 1 Draw the streamlining stripes by measuring up from the floor, and marking then drawing pencil lines. Check them with the spirit level.

STEP 2 Run masking tape around the outside edge of the lines.

STEP 3 Paint the bands of colour inside the masking tape.

STEP 4 Leave until almost dry, then peel off the tape.

MIAMI PASTEL BRIGHTS: PROJECT TWO
A piped cushion cover

YOU WILL NEED:

500mm (20in) of 1.2m (48in) width plain coloured cotton chintz per cushion

Matching coloured thread

Piped cord in a good contrasting colour (bright blue on yellow, green with pink, etc.)

Pins

Sewing machine

Cushion-making is something of a mystery until you actually make one. You then realise how much difference a fresh set of cushions can make to a room, and how inexpensive they are when you make them yourself. You also have the pleasure of choosing exactly the colours, sizes and fabrics that you most want. Make a set of different coloured cushions on the Miami colour theme, choosing four bright pastel cottons and using the main colour of each one to pipe one of the others. These cushions are simple to make and the cover is slip-stitched closed using matching thread to give a neat finish.

COLOUR KEY

1 Aqua
2 Sage
3 Bright rose pink

HOW TO DO IT

The secret of making successful piped cushions is no mystery, but you need a zipper foot on your machine so you can get up close when stitching the piping in place.

STEP 1 Fold the fabric in half and cut it into two square pieces. Pin the piping to the right side of one of the pieces, with the flat edges aligned and the cord on the inside. Snip it up to the stitch line at the corners.

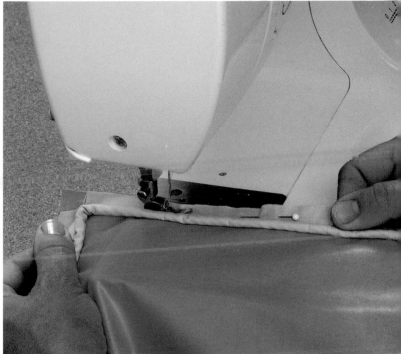

STEP 2 Stitch the piping to the fabric using the zipper foot to get right up to the cord.

STEP 3 Place the other fabric piece on top and pin it in place. Stitch it to the piped piece, once again using the zipper foot to get as close as possible to the piped cord. Leave one seam open.

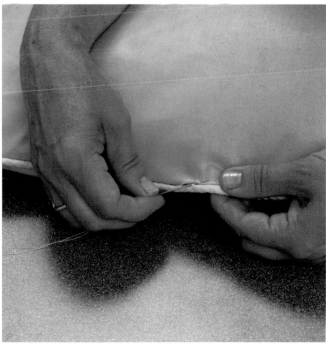

STEP 4 Turn the right way round and press lightly. Insert the cushion pad, then slip-stitch to close.

Urban natural

This is a style that has emerged from industrial chic, a 1990s phenomenon that began in New York where young people broke away from the traditional property market and moved into vacant loft and warehouse spaces. The lifestyle has spread worldwide and resulted in the regeneration of many a run-down dockland or industrial area. At first the hard-edged look was cool with plenty of open space, exposed metal beams, steel staircases and very few home comforts – but then cool started to feel a bit cold.

This is where the urban natural style comes in. Hard surfaces can be mellowed down with soft chalky distemper-based paints in natural colours. These are old-fashioned, water-based paints which can be applied directly onto brick walls or bare plaster, and being porous they allow the walls to breathe. Wooden or matting floors seem far more feet friendly when scattered with sheepskins, felt or woven rugs. Those large leather sofas can be softened with soft cashmere throws or piles of soft cushions with lamb's-wool covers. Windows are dressed down with pleated paper, calico, wooden venetian or vertical slatted blinds. Curtains are simply made from pale, plain fabrics such as loose-weave linen, fine cotton or fine voile.

Understated style

Lighting is low, subtle and ambient, concealed behind green tinted glass screens or under shelving. Scented candles, tea lights or large multi-wicked candles are a compulsory feature. House-plants contribute to the natural style so long as they also make a design statement – think orchids or sculptural desert cacti or luscious ferns.

And if the budget doesn't stretch to orchids and cashmere, we compromise and enjoy the best-looking bits of the urban natural style without losing too much sleep about whether our throws are actually cashmere or a polyester/wool mix. It's a chill-out style, where comfort is king.

Look out for mohair shawls and hand-knitted jumpers to convert into cushion covers. Large unbleached-cotton decorator's dust sheets make great curtains or sofa covers. Make use of natural textures like stone, wood, glass and leather. Stick to the key colours of dark brown, tan, mushroom, stone, olive, spring green and – beige! Avoid strong contrasts by having progressively darker or lighter shades alongside each other, so that the whole look is harmonious and easy on the eye. Repetition can look very stylish – a long galvanised metal container planted with a perfect row of African violets, for instance, or a row of pebbles on a window sill. The effect should be more meditative than passionate, creating a calm environment to ease the stresses of city living. With the background to your life in place, it's time to light a scented candle, put on some music and – relax.

URBAN NATURAL: PROJECT ONE

Painting bands of harmonious colours

YOU WILL NEED:

3 harmonious paint colours – sage green, pale coffee and light beige (chalk finish paints used here)

Decorator's masking tape

Chalk pencil

Tape measure

Straight edge with a level

Paintbrushes/roller and tray

Simplicity is the key to success in this style of decorating. It is minimalism with a soft edge, so be selective with the accessories and furniture, and make a statement on the walls. Horizontal bands of colour look best in medium- to large-size rooms, so this is a look for the living room.

The depth of the colour bands can be adjusted to make the most of your room proportions. If you have a tall room and want to bring the focus down, make the two lower bands the same size with a much wider one above. The paints used here are ideal as the chalky finish enhances the subtle colours.

COLOUR KEY

1 Coffee

2 Deep olive

3 Cream

4 Bitter chocolate

HOW TO DO IT

The secret of success is decorator's masking tape, but patience is needed as the wall must be bone dry before you apply the tape to outline the middle band of colour.

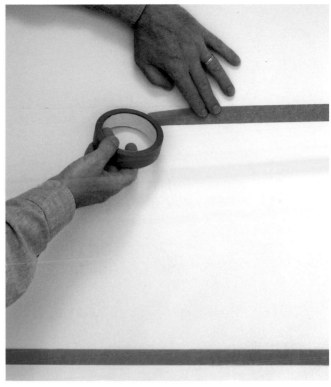

STEP 1 Divide the height of the wall by three to get three equal sized bands. Measure and mark the divisions using the tape measure, then check the horizontal with the straight edge and level, and draw soft pencil lines.

STEP 2 Run masking tape along the top of the lower line and do the same below the upper line.

STEP 3 Paint the top section of wall with light beige. Then paint the lower section of the wall sage green, slightly overlapping the masking tape so that you get a straight line when it is peeled away. Leave both to dry overnight. The paint must be bone dry.

STEP 4 Apply a line of masking tape along the top of the sage green section (if the paint is not bone dry the tape will lift the new paint). Do the same along the edge of the light beige, then paint the mid section pale coffee. When the paint is dry, peel off the masking tape.

URBAN NATURAL: PROJECT TWO
Customising a lamp

YOU WILL NEED:

A conical or cylindrical fabric lampshade

Paint in a pale coffee colour – or your choice

A brush

Bundle of bamboo from garden centre

A column-style lampbase with good wiring

Masking tape

Galvanised wire

Pliers

COLOUR KEY

1 New leaf green
2 Creamy coffee
3 Mocha
4 Chocolate

When you have a brand-new colour scheme, everything has to change, and if you are a trend-setter rather than a follower it can be difficult finding accessories to match. However, when it comes to lampshades you don't need to – just paint them with the same emulsion paint you use for the walls. It could not be simpler, and it really suits this sort of colour scheme when you are working with a limited colour palette. Once the paint is dry the lampshade can be trimmed with a darker or contrasting shade of velvet ribbon, suede fringe or textured braid. Use any lamp base – just follow the wrapping instructions.

HOW TO DO IT

Transform a boring old table lamp in an afternoon with a coat of fresh colour on the shade and a bamboo wrap around the base.

STEP 1 Clean the lampshade with a slightly damp sponge. Apply two coats of your chosen colour, being careful not to splash any inside the lampshade, which will be a special fire resistant material. Leave to dry.

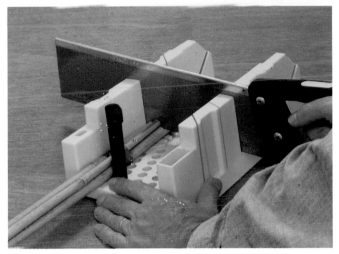

STEP 2 Tape several pieces of bamboo together and use a fine bladed saw to cut them to size. The lengths should completely cover the existing base and extend at least 50mm (2in) above it. Work out how many you need to surround the base, and cut the required amount.

STEP 3 Sand the ends then lay the pieces flat, close together and perfectly aligned. Hold them together top and bottom with a length of masking tape.

STEP 4 Wrap the bamboo around the lampbase and secure temporarily with a small piece of tape.

STEP 5 Wind the galvanised wire (rafia or twine are alternative options) around the bamboo and use the pliers to twist the ends together neatly and fold them flat against the bamboo. Do this both top and bottom, then fit the shade onto the lampbase.

Industrial modern

The industrial look is one that was born out of necessity, when young people in big cities like New York, Paris and London went looking for places to live and found themselves priced out of the market. The empty properties that attracted their attention were dockland warehouses and abandoned factories whose business had long since closed down or moved out of town to escape the traffic-clogged streets. The buildings presented an opportunity for a whole new way of living, and loft style was born.

One of the most essential aspects of industrial modern style is to retain as much of the fabric of the original building and any specialist associated material as possible. A large winch with an iron hook, for instance, would be seen as sculptural and retained, as would a metal staircase, steel shutters or a ventilation shaft. The idea is to retain the best of the building's original character, but also to make it work as a comfortable home.

Fabulous fittings

Once the factory and warehouse spaces had been colonized, the next step was to make use of factory fittings, office furniture and items of industrial scale that could be converted for use in the home. Galvanised iron shelving, movable storage units on hefty rubber casters and cafeteria tables were put to immediate use, and aluminium waste bins, metal filing cabinets, catering ovens and sets of lockers began appearing on the pages of magazines. Floors were covered with aluminium sheeting or painted with industrial paints; brickwork was exposed, and scaffolding poles were used to create mezzanine sleeping decks in the middle of vast open spaces.

Lofts and warehouses have now moved up to the top end of the market – but the industrial modern style is here to stay. Aluminium flooring, stainless steel units and catering ovens are readily available. There are aluminium and steel acrylic paints that will make any surface look like cool metal, and a range of textured wall covering that looks just like factory flooring. Metal storeroom-type shelving, track lighting and bare concrete used for seating, tables, shelving supports and planters are all a part of this pared-down style.

'Islands of comfort' are another vital ingredient – cool hard surfaces look fabulous, but everyone needs to curl up and feel warm and comfortable as well. These comfort zones are furnished with generous leather sofas, soft mohair or lamb's-wool throws, deep pile rugs and low coffee tables. Even in a vast space, clever lighting can create a sense of intimacy if kept low and concentrated by using floor and table lamps to cast warm pools of light. Use the same basic concepts to create an industrial modern style in any room – keep the style utilitarian and the space cool, open and uncluttered, but be sure to include soft areas for comfort and indulgence.

INDUSTRIAL MODERN: PROJECT ONE
Breeze-block shelving

YOU WILL NEED:

6 breeze blocks

2 x 350mm x 2m
x 20mm (14in x 6ft x
¾in) planks

Primer

Matt black paint

Paintbrush

COLOUR KEY

1 Mushroom brown
2 Mid-grey
3 Palest lemon
4 Pale mushroom

Concrete breeze blocks have replaced bricks as the basic construction material in most new houses these days. They are regular-sized, strong and inexpensive, but they don't make beautiful looking walls, so bricks are still used as a facing material. The rough grey texture of the blocks takes on a more sculptural quality when taken out of context and used indoors as shelf supports.

The planks used here are painted black wood but other materials would also look good. Glass, steel mesh or galvanised zinc are all very much a part of the industrial modern style.

HOW TO DO IT

The sculptural style of this shelving unit relies on the positioning of the breeze blocks. Use a set square to align each one at the correct angle.

STEP 1 Apply a coat of primer to the shelving planks. Leave to dry, then apply two coats of black paint.

STEP 2 Space two base breeze blocks to stand 60mm (2¼in) from the wall, 500mm (20in) apart, angled at 45° to the wall. Stand the first shelf on top with 250mm (10in) overlap at each end.

STEP 3 Place two more blocks on the shelf above the lower ones, this time angled at 90°, the narrow side facing forwards.

STEP 4 Stand the second shelf on top, again with 250mm (10in) overlap at each end, and position the final two blocks angled at 45°. Put the third shelf on top. Note: this shelving unit should only be used in rooms with solid floors and where it is unlikely to be knocked.

URBAN NATURAL: PROJECT TWO

Hardboard flooring

YOU WILL NEED:

Hardboard sheets

Panel adhesive

Tape measure

Stanley knife

Spirit level

Straight edge steel
rule

Hammer

6mm (¼in) tacks

A strip of cardboard –
shoe box type

Clear floor varnish

Foam roller and tray
or paintbrush

Hardboard has many enduring qualities which are not to be found in more modern manufactured boards. It is a kind of compressed cardboard that is rough on one side and shiny on the other.

It is inexpensive, comes in large sheets, is bendable, can be cut with a heavy-duty knife and feels warm underfoot. The brown colour deepens and can be improved with varnish.

Hardboard makes a low-budget, contemporary, industrial-style floor covering that is suitable for laying onto unattractive wooden floors or for covering shabby vinyl or even concrete.

COLOUR KEY

1 Cool grey

2 Deep ochre

3 Mud brown

4 Milk chocolate

HOW TO DO IT

Hardboard flooring is hardwearing and feels good underfoot. Using the nail guide will ensure that the lines stay straight and look decorative.

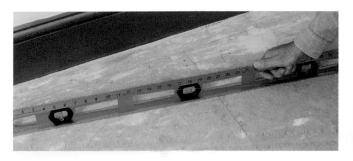

STEP 1 Make sure the existing floor is dust-free and level. Floors can be levelled with a proprietary levelling compound or with sheets of newspaper. Lay the first sheet of vinyl into one corner without adhesive to check that the walls are square.

STEP 2 Apply a long squiggle of panel adhesive to the back of the board and lay it in position. Apply foot pressure so that the adhesive grips onto the base.

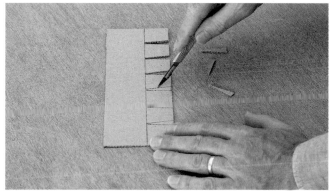

STEP 3 Butt the next sheet of hardboard up to the skirting and the first sheet. If it all fits neatly then apply adhesive and repeat the same procedure. Cover the floor in this way, measuring and making any adjustments to the final piece before laying it.

STEP 4 Decide on the width between the tacks. Mark a series of 30mm (1¼in) measurements along the straight edge of a piece of card. Cut a 50mm (2in) notch to mark each one. For a large floor you may like to widen the gap a little.

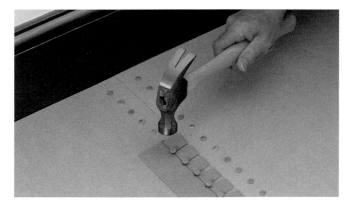

STEP 5 Line the notched edge of the card up with the edge of the hardboard and place a tack in each notch. Tap the tacks half-way in, then slide the card away and hammer the heads flush to the hardboard. This way all the tacks will line up nicely!

STEP 6 Fill the paint tray with varnish and, beginning in the far corner, apply one coat. Leave to dry, then apply a second coat.

Urban minimalist

The key elements for this look are open space, good colour and only a few well-designed pieces of furniture. Floors are left bare with either painted or waxed floorboards. Ornaments are out – instead, choose really stylish utility objects which are sculptural in their own right. We all need radiators, but the urban minimalist goes for fabulous columns, swirls or ladder-style 'rads'. Everything makes a style statement, and for this look you really do have to maintain a disciplined attitude to tidiness, because clutter is definitely out.

The furniture can be from any period so long as it is in good condition and has a design pedigree – some of the most contemporary looking chairs and loungers were actually designed in the 1920s by the famous community of designers at the Bauhaus in Germany. Chairs from any of the key decades in the last century can be reupholstered in plain contemporary colours to flatter their shape. Brand new technology sits comfortably alongside retro pieces, so long as the good design ethos remains paramount.

Urban colour

Light interiors are always enhanced when a good proportion of white is used, as it reflects and doubles the room's natural light. Leave windows bare when possible and paint window frames and surrounds white. If the windows are small then create the impression of bigger windows by painting a broad white border beyond the frames and below the sill down to floor level, which will create the impression of full length windows. Folding wooden blinds look wonderful, but if they are likely to blow the budget choose plain white blinds instead.

The urban minimalist look consists of just a few equally important elements, and colour is one of them. Consider the room's function and any existing colour that appears in furnishings, paintings or accessories when choosing a wall colour.

Adding accents

A meditative lavender or pale powder blue creates a relaxing atmosphere in a sitting room, and pale mushroom brown looks good with white and deeper browns, especially if bright colours such as spring green or red are used for upholstery. Just one or two permanent colours are needed, and others can be added as colour accents with cushions, vases or flower arrangements.

Fresh flowers are very much a part of the urban minimalist look, and a whole new style of floristry has emerged to complement it. Single variety arrangements or indoor plants are favoured, such as vibrantly red or orange dahlias in tall glass tubes; rows of pink orchids growing in moss covered containers; zinc tubs planted with white marguerite daisies or a huge earthenware pot filled with tall wild grasses.

URBAN MINIMALIST: PROJECT ONE
Floating shelves

YOU WILL NEED:

Floating shelf kit – including special fittings, screws and wall plugs

Tape measure/long ruler

Spirit level

Pencil

Drill and the correct drill bit for your wall, i.e. masonry or plasterboard

COLOUR KEY

1 Deep violet
2 Warm lilac
3 Salmon pink
4 Silver grey

The essence of this style is that rooms should appear to be more empty than they actually are. Create the impression of open space by fitting shelving that seems to float in the air without any visible support system. There are several different systems on the market that work very efficiently, so instead of 're-inventing the wheel' the project shows how to use one of the existing designs. The shelves come in a range of sizes, the one used here being the shortest. Choose a length to suit the proportions of your walls and the things you wish to display, as it is important to keep to the open uncluttered style.

HOW TO DO IT

Simple to fit and a minimalist's dream, these shelves are magical. But, as with most tricks, the explanation is quite simple.

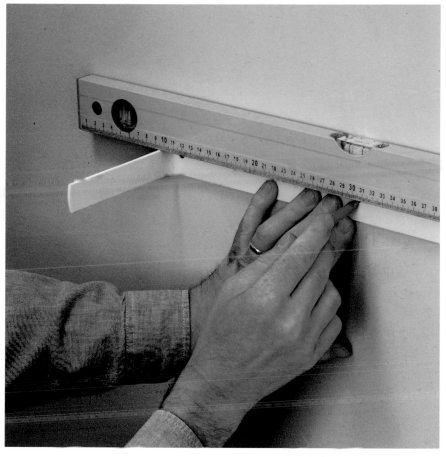

STEP 1 Having decided on the best position for the shelf, measure and mark it on the wall lightly in pencil.

STEP 2 Hold the shelf up to the wall and check it with the spirit level.

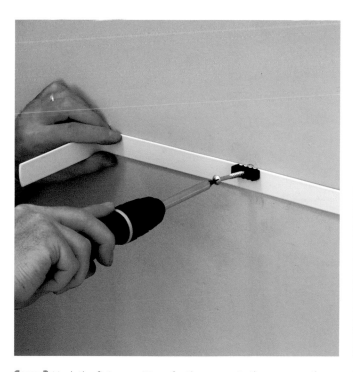

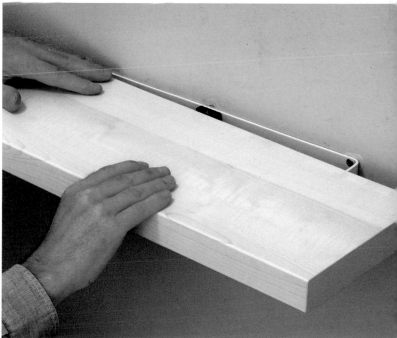

STEP 3 Mark the fixing positions for the supports then remove them and drill and plug the wall.

STEP 4 Fix the shelf onto the wall supports.

URBAN MINIMALIST: PROJECT TWO

Making a bolster cushion

YOU WILL NEED:

A bolster cushion pad

Rough silk fabric in a bold colour – enough to wrap around the body of the bolster plus two circles for the ends. Cut them to allow for a 15mm (⅝in) seam

Matching thread

Piping cord (cut a strip of fabric and fold it over the cord, then stitch close to the cord using the zipper foot, and clip along the seam allowance so the cord bends easily into a curve)

A zip to fit length

Scissors

Pins

Sewing machine

A bright silk bolster cushion on a sofa or chair can be used to add an accent of colour to the room. Bolsters are long, firm tubular cushions whose shape and proportions suit the minimalist look. They were a popular feature of the design-conscious Regency and Biedermeier styles in the 19th century, and Le Corbusier's famous leather and chrome lounger has a bolster neckrest, which certainly confers it with top design credentials.

The secret of success is to take the sewing slowly so that you keep turning the fabric in a smooth curve.

| COLOUR KEY |
| 1 Soft emerald |
| 2 Fawn |
| 3 Deep golden yellow |

HOW TO DO IT

Fit a zipper foot to the sewing machine so that you can stitch up close to the piping and the zip.

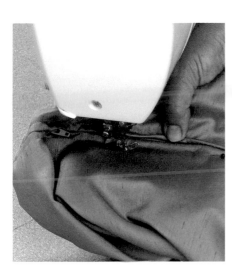

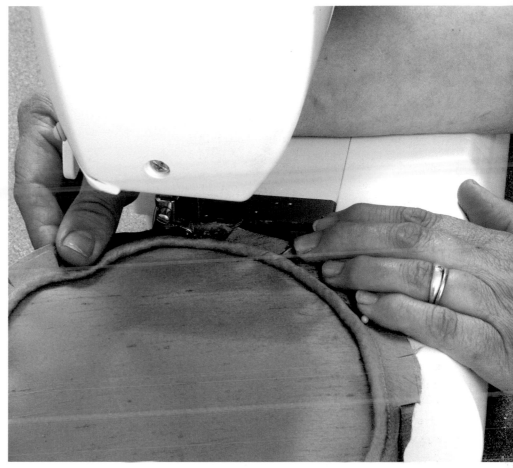

STEP 1 Turn over a small hem and stitch the zip into the seam of the main body fabric. Undo the zip so you can work on the cover.

STEP 2 Sew the piping onto the round ends before you stitch them to the main body.

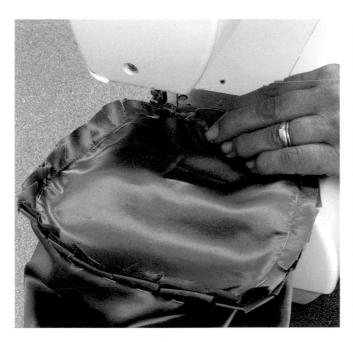

STEP 3 Snip out 10mm (³⁄₈in) notches every 30mm (1¹⁄₄in) around the end pieces. Pin the ends in place and stitch them using the zipper foot to get close up to the piping cord.

STEP 4 Press the seams lightly and turn the right side out. Fit the cushion pad inside and close the zip.

Beside the ocean

COLOUR
PALETTE

Living where the land meets the sea brings light into your life. The colour of the sea is affected by the weather – when the sun shines in a cloudless sky on a summer day it is a perfect bright blue, while on a stormy winter's day both sea and sky turn a deep grey-violet. Sunlight reflects off the sea, brightening everything along the shoreline, and there is always a holiday feeling whether the beach is soft sand, shingle or pebbles. This is what draws people to live by the sea, and the way homes are decorated reflects this relaxed feeling.

Anyone with a home overlooking the ocean will know that a room with large sea-facing windows barely needs decorating at all. What could compare to the scale of a view like that? The best you could do is have window seats, comfortable chairs, a telescope and an open fireplace for cool nights. Wherever people live near the sea they collect the treasures that come in on the tide – shells, pebbles and strangely shaped pieces of driftwood – and display them on windowsills and shelves.

Local colour

There is often a definite local style that gives a town or village a unique character. This could be the use of a limited colour palette, particular flowers in window boxes, a local stone used for house building or something ingenious like the rows of houses built from old rail carriages with added verandas on the English south coast. In places with lighthouses, fishing fleets or a strong sailing fraternity, the boat theme will never be far away, and in traditional seaside holiday towns the weatherboard huts, shops and houses with their fresh white paint and colourful window frames declare that every day is a holiday.

Coastal props

To get the look, you will need some seaside props, and the best place to find them – and the inspiration you need – is by the sea. Souvenir shops crammed with shells, anchors, buckets and spades, seagulls and sailing boats are worth investigating. A single seagull and a row of pebbles may be all your room needs to give it seaside character. Removing stones from beaches is no longer permitted, but they can be bought in garden centres. Chandlers sell everything you need for sailing, including a wonderful selection of ropes, sail cloths and eyelets. Taut steel sail cables can be used as tracks with canvas curtains, and a coil of fat rope is pure sculpture.

Choose colour to suit the location. Rooms are often painted white to make the most of the fabulous light which comes off the ocean, and this creates a brightness that works well with either primary colours or soft colours that look as if they were once bold but have faded in the sunshine. Sea greens, powder blue, sugar pink and lemon sherbet all fall into this category. Stripes, fishy prints or simple florals can all suit the seaside mood. When in doubt, let simplicity rule the day.

BESIDE THE OCEAN: PROJECT ONE
Panelling a wall with tongue and groove

YOU WILL NEED

Tongue and groove
panelling to fit
around the walls
(beaded T&G is
used here)

3 lengths of 25mm x
12mm (2in x 1in)
battens for each
wall length

Shelf 75mm x 25mm
(3in x 1in) planed
softwood to fit
around the room
(measure the length
required)

Support brackets for
shelf – to be spaced
600mm (24in) apart

6mm (¼in) wall plugs

Box of 50mm (2in)
No6 screws

Box of 25mm (1in)
panel pins

Small hammer

Drill with 6mm (¼in)
and 3mm (⅛in)
pilot bit

Fine nail punch

Mitre saw or block
with handsaw

Screwdriver

Long rule with a
spirit level

Pencil

COLOUR KEY

1 Sea green
2 Pale lavender
3 Deep sea green
4 Ice blue

Wood panelling is very much a part of beach house style, whether the home is in the Outer Hebrides or Montego Bay. The panels are light, easily transportable, simple to fit, and they cover a multitude of sins. The best thing about them, though, is the instant beach style they bring along with them. Tongue and groove can be bought in kit form or as long lengths from a timber merchant, which you can then cut down to a size to suit your room. The panelling can be fitted from floor to ceiling or, as described here, on part of the wall, topped off with a shelf to display your best beachcombing finds.

For tongue and groove panelling

Either: Measure the width of one plank and divide
this into the length of the wall area to be covered.
Multiply this figure by the height of the panelling
to find out how much wood you will need.

Or: Buy made-up panelling kits to fit the
length required.

HOW TO DO IT

Once the battens are up the panelling grows really fast. Finish it off with a shelf to hide the raw edges and display your seaside finds.

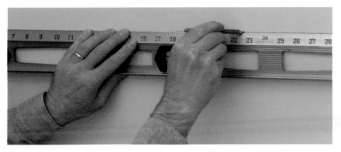

STEP 1 Remove the skirting board (to be replaced later). Measure cutting heights for all specific areas, ie below the window or above any fitted units.

STEP 2 Using the rule with the spirit level, mark three positions for the battening on the wall to align with the top, middle and bottom of the panels. Drill and insert wall plugs spaced 500mm (20in) apart then screw the battens onto the wall.

STEP 3 Beginning in one corner, place the end plank against the wall and check the vertical with the spirit level. Hammer a pin through the inside edge of the tongue, angled slightly inwards. Use the nail punch with the hammer to drive the pinhead below the surface.

STEP 4 Fit the groove of the next plank into the tongue of the first. To ensure a tight fit, place a spare piece of wood along the edge and tap it with the hammer to prevent damage to the plank's tongue. Continue in the same way to complete the panelling.

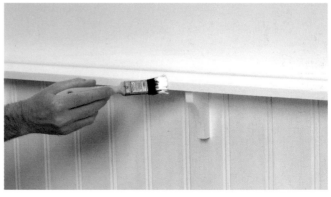

STEP 5 Cut the shelf planks to fit the wall lengths, mitring the ends for a neat fit in the corners and at any joins. Check and mark the shelf position on the wall with a spirit level. Drill pilot holes in the planks and the panels for the brackets.

STEP 6 Screw the brackets into the front of the panelling and down through the shelf into the top of the brackets. Prime and paint with gloss or emulsion sealed with marine quality varnish.

BESIDE THE OCEAN: PROJECT TWO
Curtains with eyelets

YOU WILL NEED:

Heavyweight cotton canvas

Large brass eyelets

Iron-on hemming tape

Iron-on fabric stiffener for a 100mm (4in) depth band along the top of each curtain

Scissors

Hammer

Scalpel

Pencil

Tape measure

Rope to loop through eyelets – allow about 200mm (8in) between eyelets plus an extra 150mm (6in) for a knot at each end

Extra-strong iron-on bonding tape

Curtain pole

COLOUR KEY

1 Deep orange
2 Sisal
3 Pale duck egg
4 Deep ultramarine

These stylish curtains are very easy to make, and no sewing is involved. The fabric is hemmed using an iron-on bonding tape, and the headings are strengthened with an iron-on fabric stiffener.

Once the eyelets are in place, the curtains can either be threaded straight onto a chrome rail or threaded with rope to add an extra nautical touch and suspended from any curtain pole. The eyelet fixings will need a heavyweight fabric such as cotton canvas, which will hang in neat folds when drawn back. The eyelets come in a range of sizes, as do curtain poles.

HOW TO DO IT

You need to allow plenty of time for pressing with a hot steam iron in order for the tape to bond, because the fabric is quite thick.

STEP 1 Measure the drop for the curtains, adding a 100mm (4in) turn-over at the top and 50mm (2in) to be turned up as a hem at the bottom. Press a 10mm (⅜in) fold-over along the bottom, then iron on the bonding tape to fix the hem in place.

STEP 2 Iron the fabric stiffener onto the wrong side of the curtain tops. Peel off the backing paper, then turn it down and press with a hot iron to bond the stiffened section, making a double thickness header along the top of each curtain.

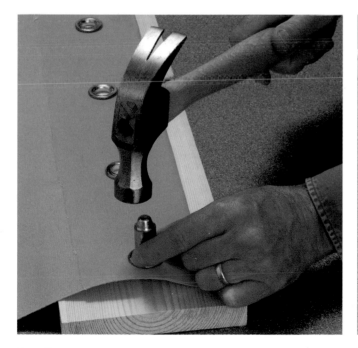

STEP 3 Mark the positions for the eyelets roughly 100mm–140mm (4–5½in) apart, depending upon the curtain width. Fix the eyelets in place using the tool, which is supplied with the pack.

STEP 4 Thread the curtains onto the pole, then arrange them to drop in neat folds.

Index

3-D effects 126–33

ACKNOWLEDGEMENTS

Special thanks go to Nicola Liddiard for design, Alistair Hughes for photography,
Lynda Marshall for picture research and Stewart Walton for styling and illustrations.

The publishers would like to thank the following for help with properties:

for Mediterranean and Chalk Collection paints (used in New Natural Room and Neutrals):
ZEST ESSENTIALS
281 King's Road, London SW3 5EW
Tel: 0207 351 7674
www.zestessentials.com

for specialist paints (used in African, Moorish, Tuscan and Provençal projects)
CASA PAINT CO. LTD
9 Bicester Road, Aylesbury, Bucks HP19 9AG
Tel: 01296 770139

for emulsion paints (used in English Country, Modern Country, Indian, Miami, Romany and Scandanavian projects)
DULUX PAINTS (all major DIY stores)
Tel: 0345 697 668

for the loan of styling properties
INTERIOR ILLUSIONS
46 High Street, Old Town, Hastings, East Sussex TN34 3EN
Tel: 01424 432524

for the shelf used in the Urban Minimalist project.
SPUR SHELVING (branches of Homebase)

The publishers would like to thank the following for the use of images:

Crown Paints: pp. 24, 43B, 55T, 78, 85B.
Elizabeth Whiting Associates: pp. 6, 15, 16, 17T, 18,
21, 25B, 26, 27T, 28, 29, 30, 33, 36, 41T, 42, 43T, 48, 49T, 51, 52, 60T, 61T, 67, 72, 73, 79B,
81, 83T, 84B, 85T, 90, 91, 95T, 96, 97, 99, 101B, 103T, 109, 144, 148, 149L, 151R, 158, 159.
GettyOneStone: pp. 12, 13TL, 39, 40, 69, 70, 71T, 82, 89T, 93, 94, 95B.
Image Bank: pp. 7, 17L, 19, 41B, 57, 58, 59, 63, 64, 65, 71B, 75, 77, 89B.
Laura Ashley Ltd 2001: pp. 11, 25T, 49B, 53T, 54, 55B, 61B, 79T, 108, 149R, 150, 151B, 152, 153B.
Next: pp. 11, 53B, 145, 153CR. **Telegraph Colour Library:** pp.13TR, 83B, 87, 88, 101T.